A Survival Guide for Teachers

A Survival Guide
for Teachers

LORI FISK
Ralph A. Gates Elementary School
El Toro, California

With the Assistance of
HENRY CLAY LINDGREN
Professor of Psychology, California State University
at San Francisco

John Wiley & Sons, Inc.
New York · London · Sydney · Toronto

To my mother, with much love,

Lori Lindgren Fisk

Library of Congress Cataloging in Publication Data:

Fisk, Lori.
 A survival guide for teachers.

 1. Teaching—Handbooks, manuals, etc.
I. Lindgren, Henry Clay, joint author. II. Title.
LB1025.2.F53   371.1'02   73-11269
ISBN 0-471-26190-4

Printed in the United States of America

10 9 8 7 6 5 4 3 2 1

Preface

One writes a manual for teachers with some trepidation these days. Everyone, it seems, has advice for them, especially people who have some special ax to grind, whether it is academic rigor and excellence, more art or more science in the curriculum, special treatment for special children, public accountability, free and open classrooms, or whatever. The advisers, every one of them sincere and dedicated and some of them eloquent, all speak in the name of children. The teacher who tries to listen to all of their demands finds herself bewildered. Even though many of the demands are contradictory and tend to cancel each other out, the net impact on the teacher is one of mingled exasperation and guilt. Inevitably she feels that she has done something serious that she should not have done, or that she has omitted some vital action that will make a crucial difference in the lives of the children who are her responsibility. It is difficult to say whether her presumed crimes of omission outweigh those of commission, or vice versa.

If these advice givers have anything in common, other than the fact that most of them have had no classroom experience, it is their tendency to overlook the fact that classrooms contain *teachers,* as well as children, and that any serious attempt to change the nature of the educational process must consider *teachers'* needs, resources, capabilities, and problems. The teacher is in the classroom, to be sure, because children need help in learning, but she is also there because she has a need to play the social roles of the teacher. In everyday language, she is there because she has something to give children. The fact that advice givers usually overlook this need may be a major reason why their advice has so little influence on teacher behavior.

vii

This advice also goes unheeded because teaching is one of the most difficult and demanding professions in the world. If done properly, it is clearly more difficult than psychiatry, for example. Both the psychiatrist and the teacher attempt to facilitate and encourage learning in some form or another, and both must cope with the emotional problems, quirks, foibles, and manipulations of the individuals they are trying to help. The teacher, however, is concerned with a much broader spectrum of learning and must see to it that children develop not only in emotional and social ways but in cognitive (skill-and-knowledge) ways as well. This complex task must be accomplished, furthermore, not with one individual at a time, but with two or three dozen or even more. If complexity of tasks performed and the degree of personal stress sustained were major factors in determining salaries, teachers would be much better paid than psychiatrists. But this is only one of many injustices that are perpetrated on teachers.

In view of the emotional stress and strain in teaching, one wonders why it is so popular. Of its popularity, there can be no doubt. As of the present moment of writing, there are literally hundreds of thousands of individuals who would leap at a chance to teach. Some are prevented from teaching because they are not legally or professionally qualified; others are qualified, but cannot teach because shortages of classrooms and funds limit the number of teaching positions than can be filled. It is patently clear that the passion to teach is one that is widespread in the population.

It is quite likely that the very demands that teaching makes on the teacher are part of the secret of its attraction. Because it is difficult, it is also interesting and challenging. As a task, it is full of the excitement of the unexpected and the resolution of uncertainties. The teacher is likely to become personally involved in both planning and carrying out her task, and also in the development of young lives. There is the opportunity to love and be loved. Few occupations, other than parenthood itself, offer such rewards.

The basic problem for teachers, the same for all who are gainfully employed, is one of maximizing rewards and eliminating, or at least minimizing, shortcomings. The problem is more crucial for teachers than for others because success becomes more precious, and failure carries with it the feeling of having let others down, particularly the children.

These feelings make the teacher more vulnerable to advice givers. Because the teacher wants so desperately to succeed, she grasps at every shred of advice, especially advice that promises to make teaching simpler than it is. The fact is, of course, that teaching cannot be reduced to a formula. It is a highly personalized endeavor, essentially creative, and even artistic. Although there are certain elements that are present in every classroom, the fact that individual teachers and students are both unique means that every teacher has to find her own way with every class. As she gets better acquainted with what to expect of herself and children in general, she becomes more skillful, senses more pitfalls and avoids them, and enjoys the sweet taste of success more frequently.

A major problem, of course, is getting through the first year or so, and this is the justification of this book. Survival during this trying period is an immensely complex problem because it involves learning a great many skills, many of them under stress situations. Not only must a teacher become familiar with a number of new roles but she must also cope with the task of getting to know herself in a new setting. If the first year is at all successful, she will also learn a great deal of practical psychology. I do not necessarily refer to techniques of dealing with others although she is bound to pick up a number of skills along this line. What I mean, instead, is that she will get to *understand* children better—that is, she will be able to predict more accurately how they will react to this or that situation, and she will learn how they view themselves, the world around them, and the significant adults in their lives. This kind of understanding is basic to success in many different kinds of human-relations jobs but is especially crucial in teaching.

Although the first year of teaching is something like life in a popcorn popper, the young teacher usually does survive, although normally there are days when she wants to give it up altogether and find something less "stimulating". Yes, most teachers survive their first year, are refreshed and restored by a summer holiday, and enter their classrooms in September a year older but a great deal wiser. During this second year, to be sure, they will make some of the same mistakes they did during the first year, but they will be less likely to be devastated by them and, as the year goes on, will make fewer and fewer of them. Getting through the first year with a whole skin, so to speak, does amazing things for one's poise and control.

Undoubtedly the first year would be much easier if teachers could learn this poise sooner and if they had a clearer grasp of their role and what they can reasonably expect from their students. Principals and supervisors know this and generally do as much as they can to reassure and suggest. Often fellow teachers are very helpful. It is in the nature of the education business, however, that principals, supervisors, or fellow teachers have pressing problems of their own and hence have little time to spare. As a result, new teachers are likely to be very much on their own, to sink or swim. It is to their everlasting credit that most of them do learn to swim and very well.

There is no doubt that teacher preparation experiences, especially practice teaching, are of great help in giving new teachers a chance to try out teaching roles and to get an idea of how classrooms and children look through the eyes of a teacher, but such preliminary experiences can only go so far. In most situations the interning teacher has someone to catch her if she stumbles or errs, and there is usually someone who can step in if chaos breaks loose. As she faces her first class on her new job, however, she is very much on her own.

This book is an attempt to help the teacher bridge this gap between training and real-life, on-the-job experience. It was written by a young woman who survived the first year very well. As a new teacher Lori Fisk was, as a matter of fact, out-standingly successful, so much so that experienced teachers who watched her felt a twinge of jealousy and wished their own first efforts had gone as well. I know, for I was one of the experienced teachers who observed her.

Her success came from four major sources, as far as I can determine.

1. She had a clear grasp of her role as a teacher. It was as though she had been practicing all her life for this role, although

she had not thought seriously about teaching until she had received her bachelor's degree in English from the University of Nevada and had found that library work was not for her.

2. The second basis of her success was her understanding of practical psychology. She knew children and what she could reasonably expect of them. She was realistic, open, and firm in the way she communicated her expectations. The children recognized her as a strong person—one who would not try to dominate them because she enjoyed the use of power but whose strength evoked feelings of confidence and security. Traditionally, teachers have been strict, often to the point of being rigid and punitive. Educators and psychologists from Pestalozzi to Carl Rogers have decried this tendency and have pleaded for consideration and more permissiveness. Misinterpretations of their viewpoint have unfortunately led to a widespread belief that "modern psychology" demands that teachers abdicate their roles and become wishy-washy nonentities. "Modern psychology" does no such thing, of course. In fact, research with children shows that adult firmness (as well as warmth) is a requisite to normal personality development and competence and that unmitigated permissiveness is detrimental. Fortunately, most teachers realize, as Lori Fisk did, that a reasonable amount of control and structure is reassuring to children and facilitates learning, and that children find classrooms confusing and distracting, when these qualities are absent.

3. Lori Fisk anticipated problems and approached them both systematically and creatively. All teachers with whom I have worked use lesson plans of some sort, but many of them regard making them as a kind of necessary nuisance at best. Lori Fisk, however, saw planning as a vital part of her program and actually enjoyed imagining the kind of problems that might occur and anticipating them. In addition, she liked to develop special projects and to find ingenious ways of capturing pupil interest and involvement.

4. Perhaps most important, she was enthusiastic. Her excitement at having the chance to teach and to work with children

in learning activities brought her through the crises, frustrations, and disappointments that are an inevitable part of the teacher's daily life. Needless to say, her enthusiasm was infectious. It is hard for a child who is ordinarily passive to resist when his teacher makes it clear that she enjoys working with him and exudes optimism about his ability to learn what is expected of him. On those occasions when she failed or made an error in judgment, she was naturally depressed, but took advantage of the situation by trying to analyze what had happened in order to determine what she could do when she encountered similar situations in the future.

There are undoubtedly other elements that contributed to her success during this first year, and these elements may occur to you as you read this book.

Because of her performance as a first-year teacher, I encouraged Mrs. Fisk to write down some of her experiences. This account served as the starting point for the present book, which also incorporates observations and analyses based on her experiences in subsequent years. In setting her experiences down on paper, Mrs. Fisk was motivated by a desire to put together a kind of handbook or guide that would enable teachers, especially those in their first year of teaching, to find ways of dealing with problems and of playing their roles more effectively. The book is obviously not a cure-all—no book can solve any individual's problems for him. But it *is* designed to be helpful, supportive, and encouraging. It is written *by* a teacher and talks directly *to* teachers who are in similar circumstances.

Although Mrs. Fisk tries to provide answers to the kind of questions and problems encountered or experienced by most teachers, she obviously does not have answers for every issue and every situation. She does not, for example, have much to say about the special problems of teachers in inner-city schools who are likely to have experiences somewhat different from those of teachers in other locations. There are, however, a number of books that speak directly to the problems of this type of teaching situation, and they are listed in the suggested readings at the end of the book. Books dealing with other special areas of interest, such as behavior modification, educationally handicapped children, and classroom management are also included there.

Even though inner-city school problems are "special," in the sense that they require techniques and approaches that do not apply in other situations, we should keep in mind that there is a kind of commonality to all kinds of teaching-learning situations. There are some basic similarities in the kinds of things teachers do in a wide variety of classroom situations, just as there are similarities in the roles played by all students, whatever their special needs may be. Furthermore, any attempts made by teachers to understand themselves and their pupils and the characteristics of their psychological environment are likely to pay off in any kind of problem situation.

My role in this book has been that of an encourager, an editor, and a psychological consultant, roughly in that order. Having urged Mrs. Fisk to write this book, I felt I had some responsibility in getting it in shape to be published. I therefore took on the task of organizing and editing her material, changing the order of the presentation, writing a "bridge" here and there for smoothness, and the like. I tried to leave the Lori Fisk style alone, however, and we are both convinced that her message comes through as she wanted it to. In a couple of places I added a paragraph or two to bring out some psychological point that I thought needed stressing. All in all, I would say that the book is about 90 percent Fisk and 10 percent Lindgren.

I hope you will enjoy reading it as much as I did editing it.

Lori Fisk expresses her appreciation for the help she received from Mr. Arnold Berman, Principal, and from Mrs. Shelley Brooks, her fellow teacher and friend, during her years of teaching at Gates School, El Toro, California. We also thank the people whose encouragement and suggestions were helpful in the several revisions of the manuscript: Mrs. Mary Stoddard, Principal of the Fremont School, Carson City, Nevada; Dr. Laurel Tanner, Associate Professor of Curriculum and Instruction, School of Education, Temple University, Philadelphia; Dr. everett T. Keach, Jr., Department of Social Science Education, The University of Georgia, Athens, Georgia; Dr. Kopple C. Friedman, Chairman-Division of Professional Studies, Richmond College of the City University of New York, Staten Island, New York; Dr.

xiv   preface

John McNeil, Department of Education, University of California, Los Angeles, Los Angeles, California; and Dr. Eveleen Lorton, Associate Professor of Education, University of Miami, Coral Gables, Florida.

Thanks also go to Lorraine Sevo for her help in typing the manuscript, and special thanks go to Fredi Lindgren, for her editorial assistance as well as for her contributions as a psychologist and a former elementary school teacher.

HENRY CLAY LINDGREN

**California State University
at San Francisco**

Contents

1

how teachers (and students)
can win (or lose)

There is a great deal of disagreement today about what schools should be or not be or what they should do or not do, but there is one thing that everyone is agreed on: schools exist so that children may learn. The fact that so many children do not learn, or seem to be learning the wrong things, is what much of the fuss is about.

If children do not learn, schools have failed, and our investment of labor, anxiety, hope, and tax monies have been in vain. And when schools fail, or seem to have failed, everyone looks for someone to blame—usually the teacher, because it is the teacher who is the key person in the process of translating this economic and psychological investment into results in the form of children's learning. Often, as I face the 30-odd children in my classroom, I am aware that the success or failure of their educational program rests on my shoulders, and it is not a comfortable feeling. At such times, I think, how much easier it would be if there were only 20 or even a half-dozen children in the class. Then the job would be simpler, and I could give more individualized attention to their problems and potentialities as learners. This is only a dream, of course; the inescapable reality is that there are 30 eager and uneager learners facing me, and tomorrow there may be more.

I think, too, that what a teacher needs in order to deal with this many-headed problem is a mixture of energy, enthusiasm, creativity, empathy, ego strength, firmness, charisma and, heaven knows, how many other qualities besides. Although no one can say which of these qualities is the most important, one thing is certain: no matter how much a teacher has to offer, she is not going to be very successful unless she can have some kind of noticeable effect on the behavior of the children placed in her charge. And the precondition that enables her to be effective is control.

CONTROL: THE VITAL INGREDIENT

Control is a troublesome concept for today's teacher who wants desperately for children to learn to be creative, independent, and mature. It seems that in order to achieve these desirable goals, control would be the last thing that children need. Yet in order for children to develop the hoped-for qualities, they must begin their learning in a situation that is not distracting, a situation in which they can focus on the kind of activity that leads to being able to function independently. They cannot do this in the chaotic anarchy that often results when groups of children are thrown on their own. By starting in an ordered or controlled situation, children can be helped to learn the skills and attitudes they need to function independently, at which point adult control can gradually fade into the background to be replaced by the child's inner controls as reinforced by peer control.

Control cannot be an end in itself, and the ability to control a group of children is nowhere near the most important skill of an effective teacher. But it is a starting point for the learning that is to follow.

LOST: ONE FOURTH-GRADE CLASS

How important is control? You don't know until you've lost it. We are entering a fourth-grade classroom anywhere in the United States. It is 2 P.M. in late September. The subject at hand is math. The teacher is young, eager, and inexperienced. She is full of beautiful philosophy gleaned from education courses at the state university. She wants to inspire, to enthrall, to truly teach. But here's what is happening.

Several children are giggling in the back of the room. A note reading "Billy loves Sandy" has just been passed from Judy to Kurt to Karen on its meandering way across the room to Tammy. Roger is looking out the window wishing he were fishing with his Uncle Mike. Robert is surreptitiously carving grooves inside his desk, and he holds the rapt attention of Hilario and Willie who sit on either side of him. Rhonda and Marney are coloring the letters on the dittos given to them in Health Education by the school nurse. Billy is peeling back his bandaid to inspect an infected cut for the 13th time this afternoon. His neighbors are looking on with horrified interest. At the front of the room surrounded by chalk, flannel-board cutouts, a teacher's guide and other instructional paraphernalia, stands Miss Goodheart. She believes she is instructing the middle-ability math group on the subject of joining and separating sets, but she is mistaken. She is talking to a brick wall.

Miss Goodheart asks, "How many objects are in this set?" She places felt cutouts of apples on the flannel board. She looks up expectantly, waiting for hands to wave in the breeze. There are none. No one is listening. She raises her voice. "I said, 'How many objects are in this set?' Children! Aren't you listening? Don't tell me nobody knows the answer."

The 10 children near the front of the classroom are staring blankly at Miss Goodheart. The rest of the middle-math group is occupied as previously described. Conversations begin to sprout around the room. Three boys begin to make rude noises. The volume of sound rises, and the voices of the children overpower the voice of Miss Goodheart.

"Boys and girls!" she shouts desperately. "Boys and girls!"

A buzzer signals the end of the math period. Miss Goodheart admits defeat publicly. "Oh, no! I don't have time to explain page 19, so we'll have to do that tomorrow."

"No homework, yay!" shouts one boy.

The cheers of rejoicing are taken up by several other children. Miss Goodheart is on the verge of tears. The children obviously have the upper hand. She is not inspiring, enthralling, nor truly teaching. She is losing. Thirty-nine 10-year-old children have outsmarted her and prevented her from playing her proper role (teacher) by refusing to play their roles (learners).

During recess, Miss Goodheart sits forlornly at her desk and tries to analyze the situation. Where did she go wrong? Why don't the children like her? Why won't they listen to her? She feels very guilty about the wasted math period, embarrassed at her failure, and fearful of facing the youngsters tomorrow.

THE TEACHING-LEARNING GAME

After school, Miss Goodheart is brooding over a cup of tea in the teacher's room. She might have spent the rest of her teaching career brooding over cups of tea if Mr. Mach had not come in then. Mr. Mach had a reputation that was almost legendary. Children crowded around him when he walked across the playground, and it was rumored that even the principal consulted him about problem cases.

Ordinarily Mr. Mach's entrance would have caused Miss Goodheart to brighten up, but today she was too depressed. Mr. Mach could see that something was amiss, so he said nothing until he had poured himself a cup of coffee and sat down. After a minute of silence he asked:

"Something wrong, Miss G.? Kids getting you down?"

Miss Goodheart nodded.

"What's the problem?" he asked, encouragingly. "Anything I can do to help?"

Miss Goodheart's first impulse was to say "No," but then she blurted out: "How do you make them pay attention and stop talking?"

"Just one or two kids?" he inquired.

"No," she admitted shamefacedly, "the whole class."

Mr. Mach laughed. "Oh, I see. It was circus time in Room 13, and the animals were getting out of hand. Tell me about it."

So Miss Goodheart recounted the events of her abortive math lesson, sparing no details. She finished by asking:

"Where did I go wrong? Why didn't they listen to me?"

"Because you were not playing the game," he replied.

Miss Goodheart was perplexed. "What do you mean—the game?"

"Why, the Teaching-Learning Game, of course? Don't you see the comparison? The Teaching-Learning Game is just like any other game, like chess, or softball, or bridge, except that both sides can win and both can lose. It has sides and rules, too."

"Tell me more," said Miss Goodheart, fascinated.

"Let's put it like this," said Mr. Mach, settling back for a good, long talk, "you can win this game, Miss Goodheart, but first you have to control the situation."

There are two sides in the classroom game, Mr. Mach told her: teacher and student. They can either work together harmoniously to a common end (learning), or they can work against each other when each group desires different goals. An example of the latter would be Miss Goodheart's situation, in which her goal was learning, and the children's goals were something other than learning. Unwritten rules govern the Teacher-Learner Game, Mr. Mach said, rules that were internalized by children even before their school career begins. These rules govern behavior patterns for both teachers and students.

Then Mr. Mach took a close look at the rules and behavior patterns that were operating in Miss Goodheart's situation, so she could discover just where she lost the class.

The rules were broken when Miss Goodheart became so involved and caught up in her own performance that she failed to be fully aware of what her students were doing and how they were responding. Mr. Mach pointed out that a teacher must be able to read subtle body cues and facial expressions that tell him "I don't understand" or "I am bored—involve me."

Miss Goodheart's pupils conveyed this message to her by giggling in the back of the room, passing notes, and engaging in other nonlearning behavior. Had she played the game properly she would have seen frowns, noses quizically screwed up, and eyes clouded over by lack of comprehension. She should also have noticed that Hilario and Willie were looking into Mike's desk and that Rhonda and Marney were writing. These signals should have alerted her to the fact that some of her students were not understanding her presentation, and that she needed to get their interest and attention back through rephrasing or re-presenting concepts. However, she failed to pick up the cues and signals that her students were sending her.

The fourth-graders' game playing had a number of implications, Mr. Mach said. For one thing, their motivation was very complex. Some of the children were trying to convey to their teacher that they found her presentation unclear, whereas others were more interested in engaging her in a battle of wits through which they hoped to grab control right out of her hands. They were curious to see just how much fidgeting, playing, and chattering they were able to get away with and were also attempting to set the tone for the remainder of the school year *on their terms*. They were saying, in essence, "Teacher, you may talk and play at teaching us all you wish, but we are not going to interact with you as learners. These are examples of the kind of behavior we plan to indulge in this year. Are you going to agree to these terms or do you plan to force us to comply with your terms?"

By the time Miss Goodheart tried to take control of her class at the end of the period, it was too late. When Miss Goodheart raised her voice in an attempt to gain control, the children knew exactly what she was doing. The tone of desperation in her voice was obviously a distress signal. They could see that their opponent was down and failing fast, and they took advantage of her confession of weakness by escalating their efforts. When the buzzer sounded, they were clearly the victors.

MIXED MOTIVES IN THE CLASSROOM GAME

We will leave Miss Goodheart and Mr. Mach at this juncture and take a look at some of the motives underlying the childrens' role in the Teaching-Learning Game. In typical classroom situations, children are torn between two sets of motives. One is the desire to learn. Every child (whether he realizes it or not, and it is up to the good teacher to make him realize it) truly wants to learn and become more mature. It is a natural, basic, human need. Some psychologists feel it is practically a biological drive! Children are, however, also motivated by a desire not to learn but feel compelled to remain childish, impulse ridden, and even infantile at times. They want desperately to grow up, but it is such hard, uphill work! Hence there are times in the lives of children (and adults too) that they do not want to learn at all. At such times, they are very vulnerable to distractions and will behave in ways that tend to impede the learning process. It is also no secret that the desire to learn and become mature varies in intensity from person to person. Some children are more interested in learning and becoming mature than others.

In other words, learning can be fun, but it can also be very demanding. Learning is natural, basic, and exciting and most children truly enjoy it, but it does require concentration, thinking, puzzling, and tuning out distractions.

WHO WINS—IN THE END?

Why should the teacher call the shots? Why should she win the Teaching-Learning Game? Why can't the children be allowed to win the game of control?

Because when the teacher wins, everybody wins. When control reigns in a classroom, learning is going on. Most of the children are happy and contented under these circumstances, and those who are momentarily (we hope) uninterested in learning are at least not interfering with the majority who are actively engaged in the learning process. When the children win the control game, everybody loses. Learning does not take place; the teacher is prevented from carrying out her role as instructor; and the children are prevented from playing their roles as learners.

2

games children play

If you are a beginning teacher and are about to face your class for the first time, it is important to remember that the children are far ahead of you in playing classroom games, because they have had more extensive and more recent experiences than you have. Furthermore, they seem to be more aware of the possibilities in the Teaching-Learning Game than young teachers are. For one thing, they have more confidence and are surer of the support of their fellow class members, whereas you are going to face them alone and, if you are like most of us, are not sure whether you can live up to your own expectations, let alone theirs.

The week before I started my student teaching, waves of panic swept over me, momentarily quenching the glow of self-confidence that I had been working to keep lit during the months of course work that had preceded. The closer the first day came, the more I was convinced that I would be unable to handle student teaching at all, so I sought the nearest authority figure, who happened to be my educational psychology professor. I told him of my doubt that I would be able to do anything with the sixth grade that had been assigned to me. Although I had several successful experiences previously in working with children, I was suddenly quite afraid of them. I was convinced they would make mincemeat out of me in five minutes.

The professor listened patiently and then tried to snap me out of this depressed frame of mind. Whenever I begin to feel the least bit frightened of children, which incidently still happens on occasion, I think of his comments.

"Don't forget, they are *children*," he said. "You are an *adult*. This gives you an automatic advantage right from the start. Although they will probably test and challenge you, they will look up to you. They expect you to be in charge, and they will accept you in that role."

"Besides," he continued," you know so much more than 11-year-olds, and they know that you know more than they do."

I repeated this litany several times during the week before my student teaching began. I made a shy beginning with those sixth-graders, but I was definitely not overwhelmed by fear.

A POSITIVE NOTE

Most children do not view their teacher as a mortal foe. Children who do will be dealt with later on in this book. The majority of children accept and expect discipline and, after their first month of kindergarten, realize that there will be rules in their classroom that they will be expected to follow.

It is also important to realize that most children in elementary school expect to like and respect their teacher. This gives you an advantage. The fact that most children have these positive feelings, however, does not preclude the possibility that they will try to get away with as much as they possibly can. It is normal for children to test school and classroom rules in order to find out whether adults mean what they say. Sometimes this testing is pushed to the teacher's breaking point and even beyond. The fact the children want and expect discipline and to like their teacher, but at the same time try her patience, only shows that they are human (and inconsistent) and probably are only behaving like the adults they admire and imitate. When this occurs, it is important for you to realize that this behavior is usually not meant personally.

Children also test the limits with adults because it is the natural tendency of a child to challenge all authority figures. Children do this with their teachers, their parents, their scout leaders, their babysitters, and almost everyone over the age of 15. When I was a child, I felt as if childhood was a time in your life when grown-ups told you what to do, when to do it, and what to do when you finished doing it. I could hardly wait until I grew up and could tell people what to do, too. (Small wonder

I became a teacher.) I was not a "problem" child and almost always did as I was told, sometimes even cheerfully. But I still did my testing and challenging, just like any other child.

It's Harder To Cope, These Days. Teachers of the past did not have as many control problems as teachers do today. Parents nowadays often remind you of this, expecially when you are having difficulty with their child! Most of us who are beginning teaching today remember schools as being stricter and more authoritarian than the ones in which we teach today. When I was a child, there were dire consequences when rules were broken, and many of my classmates were sent down to the principal's office where, on occasion, they were paddled.

I recall one scene in the fifth grade when the principal suddenly darted into the back door of the classroom and slapped a boy who happened to be drawing pictures on his desk while other children were filling out their workbooks. And most of us remember children being stood in the corner, humiliated by tongue lashings, and even being spanked by teachers. Most of us, in other words, were taught at some time or other by individuals who inspired more fear than interest in learning.

Schools nowadays have fewer unreasonable and unbending rules and are more flexible than they used to be. To be sure, many critics of education believe that today's schools are repressive, authoritarian, and stifle creativity. It is not the purpose of this book to answer such critics but, even if they have a point, we must all admit that schools emphasize classroom control and discipline measures far less than they used to.

Today's student is also somewhat different than the elementary school child of yesterday. He is more vocal in his complaints and criticism of adults, authority, and the "system." He is much more likely to express his opinions, and his home training reflects a general trend in the direction of permissiveness. This is not to say that the majority of our students have been raised in an atmosphere of total absence of discipline. I merely wish to point out that times have changed in the direction of freedom, and that children have changed with the times.

GAMES CHILDREN PLAY WITH TEACHERS: HOW TO RECOGNIZE THEM AND DEAL WITH THEM

I noted earlier that children, regardless of the fact that their motives are usually good, are going to involve you, their teacher, in many situations that will be nerve-racking and can interfere with your control of your class.

Children have an arsenal of techniques that they use to get something they want. What they want is usually more than you are willing or should be willing to give them at the moment. Occasionally what they want is to annoy or harrass you into relenting and giving them what they know they should not have. The rare, straightforward child will make a direct request ("Can we go out to recess ten minutes early today?") and will accept your refusal with a good-natured nod only slightly tinged with disappointment. This section of the book would not be necessary if all children were straightforward and above-board in their methods. Most children, consciously or unconsciously, are devious. Fortunately, however, their strategies can be easily recognized. Once alerted to what is really going on, you can "take steps." Forewarned is forearmed.

The High-Pressure Technique. The operational premise of the High-Pressure Technique is, "If we ask her often enough, she's bound to give in."

The annoying truth about the High-Pressure Technique is that children would not use it so frequently if it didn't work. The High-Pressure Technique obviously works on their parents and grandparents so, equally obviously, why not try it out on Miss Nice-Gal, my teacher? After all, she is a grown-up just like my mother.

Children get field training in the art of applying pressure at an early age. Picture the following situation: here's frantic Mommy bustling around to get her dinner on the table before Daddy gets home from work. Little James decides to ask for a cookie. He knows in advance that Mommy will say, "No, you can't have one." He knows this because it has often been made clear that cookies are for after dinner and Mommy has often explained the evils of Spoiling One's Appetite. If James is capable of comprehending the intricacies of high finance, Mommy has explained to him the evils of Large Dental Bills (and Large, Nasty Cavities). Furthermore, to make requests while Mommy is scurrying around the kitchen is really very dirty pool. But he asks anyway. Big Surprise, Mommy says "NO!" James asks again making his little voice more plaintive and more demanding. Mommy says "NO" again, and her voice is a little sharper as she looks at the clock and estimates that dinner will be 15 minutes late. James keeps it up and asks and asks until finally, desperately in hopes of getting the kid out of her way and dinner on the table, Mommy says, "All right, *take* a cookie! But just this once!"

Mommy may think she is bribing James to stay out of her way when she is cooking. But no. Mommy is TEACHING James to make a blooming nuisance of himself until he gets what he wants. Mommy is also teaching James that an adult "No" is an invitation to be pressured—a signal that continued, insistent demands will lead to surrender. It may take several tries but don't give up, James old boy. You'll get your cookie eventually.

When our friend James is in elementary school, he will be putting his learning to good use, especially if his teacher is a woman, because then she is more like Mommy. Unless Daddy succumbs to high pressure, James won't be as likely to try this one on a male teacher. (But don't count on this, gentlemen.) James will ask his kindergarten teacher several times in a successively whinier voice whether he can hold the class guinea pig during music ("Teacher, can I hold Snowflake when we're singing?" "No, James, you know we only take the guinea pig out of its cage during activity time.") If you are James' smart kindergarten teacher, you will hold your ground and refuse to succumb to his persistent requests.

Now James is in the fifth grade and he wants to know if he can stay at his seat and do clay instead of coming to his reading group. Why, you ask, is James still using the high-pressure technique since all his teachers beginning with kindergarten probably refused to honor his outrageous requests? Why? Because (1) it is still working on Mommy or (2) somewhere along the line, one of his teachers occasionally GAVE IN. This is the isolated incident that he remembers. He forgets all the other times it didn't work. As my principal so aptly puts it, "Children are optimistic gamblers."

What can you do about this? Keep refusing, kindly and firmly. This is not as easy as it seems because you are a nice teacher. A nice teacher likes to please her children. And honestly, you and I don't really like to say "No" to a child. After all, we rationalize, he must really want to do this since he keeps asking me about it. Maybe he isn't allowed to do anything he wants at home. Maybe I should be nice to him and say "Yes." Maybe nobody else does.

But restrain yourself. Now is not the time to say "Yes" to him. Say "Yes" when his request is reasonable. If you let yourself feel guilty about refusing outrageous or irrelevant requests, you have lost the first set and are on the way to losing the whole game. Just keep turning thumbs down to his high pressuring and maybe, by the end of the year, James will have figured out that when you say "No" that you mean "No" the first time. And look at it this way: your firmness will help next year's teacher have an easier time of it with your persistent little friend.

Many adults justify giving in to the High-Pressure Technique when they grant the child's request, qualifying it with "Just this once." There is no chance that a child will accept these words at face value. "Just this once" is universally taken by children to mean something wildly different from what adults believe it does. It means, "Just this once, and hopefully, also the next hundred times I ask for it!" A teacher who relents "just this once" will be facing nine months of painful vulnerability. The children will never allow her to forget what she allowed them to do "just that once."

"But Miss Nice-Gal," they will chorus, "last month you let us chew gum in class."

"Now, boys and girls," replies Miss Nice-Gal, "remember I told you it was just for that one time."

Miss Nice-Gal hopes the subject is closed but she will, to her sorrow, learn otherwise because she will periodically be reminded of that fatal day when she let the little darlings chew gum. She has opened Pandora's Box. I opened it one year when

I should have known better by allowing my children to finish up some Christmas gifts during our reading period. I explained to them, naturally, that we were only doing this because we were falling behind and had to finish our angels before vacation. We obviously couldn't give our mothers their Christmas presents in January, so we had to use some reading time to complete them. So guess who was asked at least biweekly during the following six months if unfinished art projects could be finished during reading? "After all, Mrs. Fisk, we did it at Christmas! So why not now?" My class was composed of 31 reasonable and fairly mature children. But, as you can see, they were most definitely children.

The "I'm-Only-an-Innocent-Bystander" Technique. Whenever a fight, rock-throwing incident, or careless classroom accident occurs, up pops the Innocent Bystander. Before you attempt to settle the incident, you must first find out who was actually involved in it. Then you should remove the guilty ones to a quiet corner of the room, take them outside the door, and make an appointment to discuss the problem at the next recess or after school. However, getting to this point is half the fun, as far as the children are concerned. When a problem has occurred on the playground, you have the further disadvantage of not having seen it unless, of course, you were on playground duty. Let us say that you were not on the playground and that now comes the problem of sorting it out. When your children come to the line after recess, they greet you with agitated frenzy, everyone talking at once.

"Bill threw a rock at me!" one of the girls cries.

"I did not," says Bill.

"Oh, yes you did," says another girl, or perhaps a boy who would like to see Bill get in trouble.

"All right," you say, "who was there when the rock was thrown?" (Notice that you have not directly accused Bill as yet.)

Thirty hands go up. A few more questions and a few more chaotic, shouted responses, charges, and countercharges. But it is not complete chaos. By putting together what you know about your class with what you are sorting out, it begins to dawn on you that Bill Frank, Steve, and Roy were throwing rocks at Jane, Shelley, Cathy, and Linda, who instigated the rock throwing by taking the football away from the boys.

Now we need to determine which children were playing the role of ringleader in both groups. You might have a clue to the ringleader's identity, based on what you remember of each of the participants in the fray. But what if this happens in September, before you really know what kind of playground conduct to expect from each one of these children? Even in May, your hunch might be wrong. So bear this in mind: there is most likely one ringleader and countless others who egged him or her on. The "egger-oners" are the ones who are going to adopt the role of Innocent Bystander. First, the Innocent Bystander admits that he or she was indeed THERE. He saw everything that happened—in living color. He was going to tell the teacher on duty, he tried to stop it, he was just on his way to tell the principal when the bell rang, and so on. But, alas, circumstances prevented him from doing anything but stand there and watch Cathy grab the football and kick Frank in the shins or watch Steve pick up that rock and hurl it at Linda.

At this point you tell the children in a firm, no-nonsense voice that the subject is closed and will be discussed later. This usually holds them. They are reassured that the teacher is going to do something about it. You are also giving yourself enough time to plan strategies and think through ways of handling the situation once you've settled it.

It is now the next recess and you are sitting in your classroom with the eight offenders. All eight are Innocent Bystanders. What you discover is that you have programmed yourself for 15 more minutes of charges and counter-charges, accusations, denials, and excuses. I have found that the best way to avoid this mess is not to have a group session but to question each participant privately. Such an approach makes things much easier on the child, for one thing. If he knows who started it, he can tell you personally, without fear of being branded as a tattletale or, worse yet, being whomped after school.

After you have listened to the eight versions, you will know who is guilty of first-degree rock throwing or football stealing, and who were the accomplices after the fact. But you do not tell the assembled group of eight who was guilty. You do tell ALL of them that this sort of behavior is not what is expected of fourth-graders or first-graders on the playground, and that you sincerely hope it will not occur again.

Unless there were injuries, and particularly if this were the first time such an incident has happened, I would leave it at that. I would also make it clear that if the incident occurs again, firmer measures will be taken. You don't have to specify what measures. If any one of the children is foolish enough to do this again, he will find out. Perhaps your school has a specific list of offenses and punishments, varying with the number of times the misbehavior has occurred. Maybe your school has a general plan that you are supposed to follow in dealing with chronic rock-throwers. The majority of schools do not have such well-defined procedures, so you will have to develop your own. I will fill you in on my system a bit later, so just sit tight. Make it clear that you consider EVERYONE guilty, even if they didn't actually throw a rock. You might discuss with them the wrongness of encouraging somebody to do something that everyone knows is bad. Psychologists call this *peer-group pressure*, and it is a very powerful force to cope with.

Most misbehavior occurs in groups, and the older the child, the more vulnerable he is to such peer pressure. Even a child who is usually well-behaved can be coerced into misbehavior by his friends and classmates, especially if one of the instigators is a well-liked and popular child. Sometimes the pressure of only one peer will do the trick. I encouraged a very upstanding friend to smoke a cigarette when we were both 13. I'm sure she would never have dreamed of such an evil thing had I not applied the pressure, and I wouldn't have done it by myself either.

Feigned Innocence. Most adults are aware that ignorance of the law is not considered a valid defense. However, adults swear up and down to the policeman who is giving them a speeding ticket that there was no sign posting the speed limit, or if there was, they just didn't see it and, therefore, didn't know. They will also tell the policeman that now that they know,

they will never do it again. It is no wonder that feigned innocence is used by children also. They pick up this from their
elders.

I always make a point of going over all school and classroom
rules in detail during the first and subsequent days during the
first week of school. Every time I make an assignment, I go
through the litany of how I want it done, how much freedom I
will allow (you can either make a poster or a diorama), and what
should be done with the assignment when it is completed.
(Keep it in your desk, put in on the bookcase, lay it on my desk,
etc.) You do this because children like and need well-defined
situations and want to know what is expected of them.

You also do this because you want to close the door on
Feigned Innocence. If you make a point of making your children
aware of requirements, you will save yourself that fleeting instant of doubt when you are confronted with "But I didn't know
we weren't supposed to play on the kindergarten's swings at
recess." If this is a school rule, and you have gone over the rules
with your class, you won't be thinking, "Good grief. I guess I
didn't mention the swings!"

The more ridiculous the protestations of the child who claims
he didn't know, the more likely the rest of the class will be to
take your part. So when Greg tells you with an air of wronged
soul that he didn't know he was supposed to come to line when
the recess was over, the rest of the class will chorus, "No way,
Greg, Miss Nice-Gal told us."

Greg may try to save face by claiming he must have been
absent that day, but you and he and everyone else knows he
was here. He is either fudging or he had temporarily discon-
nected his ears while you were expounding on the standards for
proper recess conduct.

You reply, "I guess you forget this time, Greg, but try to
remember in the future that you must come to line when you
hear the bell."

Unless Greg is totally absent-minded, he will come to line
after the next recess. This will not stop him, of course, from
"forgetting" other rules and feigning innocence when caught.
The only time your whole class will feign innocence is when the

rules were not clear, or when all of them have broken a rule as a body.

A variation of this theme is the legalistic Feigned Innocence technique. The child who practices this sort of maneuver is the child who would have to be told, "Please don't eat the daisies." He presumes that unless an action has been expressly forbidden, it is okay. This child would like you to turn into a drill sergeant. That way, he would not have to make his own decisions, and he would have a good excuse for fearing you or even disliking you. But mostly he doesn't want to strain his brain by having to make intelligent decisions. His excuse, of course, is always, "But you never told us not to do it!" My reply is, generally, "But I shouldn't HAVE to tell you. You should be able to figure it out on your own."

One of my bête-noires one year was exactly this type of child. He envisioned himself as Mr. Cherub who never, never did anything that the teacher told him not to do. In my classroom there are only a few rules, because I believe in developing critical thinking in children by allowing them to make as many of their own decisions as if feasible. I do not believe solving all possible issues for them and holding their hands every inch of the way.

Mr. Cherub did not like this policy, and he tried to sabotage it at every turn, desperately eager to abdicate all personal responsibility for the comfort or welfare of others. When he unplugged the earphones of other children as they were listening to a reading tape he said, "But you never told us not to!" When caught writing on his desk with an indelible felt-tip pen—you guessed it: "You never told us we couldn't do it!" Actually, it took several months before I managed to convince Mr. Cherub that a reasonably intelligent lad like himself was certainly able to realize that he shouldn't do some things even if I hadn't specifically told him he couldn't. It was steady, uphill work for both of us, and I attained success only by praising him every time he used his head.

Sowing Seeds Of Insecurity. This technique is reserved for use on inexperienced teachers. If you are inexperienced, they figure, they can probably get away with more. It is also used with teachers who are new to a particular school. Actually, the child has no way of knowing whether or not you have taught before. If you weren't at his school last year, he starts testing you in the hope that you may be inexperienced. Hence it is wise to mention your previous "classes" (i.e., your student teaching, but don't call it that), but also be sure that your present group of children is being compared very favorably.

As a beginning teacher, or one who is new to a school, you are at a disadvantage. The children know more about the school rules and procedures than you do, and you can count on them to lead you down the primrose path when they get the chance. School policies are quite complex, and they operate at several levels, official and otherwise. It takes even an experienced teacher some time to figure out the way things are done at a new school. There are written rules, covering such things as playground procedure and behavior and, also, teaching behavior. There are also customs or rules that are unwritten, but which everyone on the staff seems to know about. Nobody tells you about these unless you ask specifically. But a new teacher does not want to make a nuisance of himself by asking the principal for clarification on procedures five times a day and, furthermore, it is considered up to the teacher to find out how things are done. The office staff and school secretary are often helpful, but it is a good idea to check out what they tell you about interpretations of school rules. This will save you from many embarrassing blunders. Yet it is tempting to relax, especially if you have never taught before. Furthermore, as a new teacher, you want to appear tolerant and accepting, so if a child tells you something that sounds reasonable, your impulse is to believe him.

One school I taught in had an unwritten law about chewing gum in class. Nowhere in the printed list of rules could I find anything about whether or not students could chew gum in class. During my first year of teaching, some children solemnly assured me that last year Mrs. Real-Nice permitted gum chewing. The children who had been in Mr. Good-Guy's class also claimed that he allowed gum chewing if the chewer provided gum for other children. The pupils who had Miss Pleasant claimed they couldn't remember, but if they really thought it over, maybe they *did* get to chew gum. (Perhaps you feel that lengthy discussions of the pros and cons of gum chewing are ridiculous, but it is often the seemingly petty and small concerns that can drive you up the proverbial wall and set you up as a pushover in the children's eyes.)

After some sorting out, I discovered the following facts: 1. Mrs. Real-Nice had a hard-and-fast, no-gum-in-class rule. Hence she only "permitted" the gum chewing that she did not catch. "After all," reasoned her ex-students, "if some of us chewed gum for two days and she didn't see it, then weren't we allowed to chew gum?" 2. Mr. Good-Guy said that he had on one occasion permitted his children to indulge themselves in gum when a child showed up with 28 pieces. It was on the last day of school, he thought. 3. Miss Pleasant had transferred to another school, but I did unearth the sorry truth (sorry to the children) that she had personally removed every piece of gum that found its way into each of her charges' mouths.

Very interesting! I still do not have any strong feelings about gum or no gum, but I did feel that the janitor might like me better if he didn't have to scrape wads of used gum off the floor. Hence I had decided before I started teaching to ban gum in the classroom. However, because I was a teacher new to my school, I also wanted to be consistent with the way the gum problem was handled at my school, so I asked the other teachers what they did about gum. What eventually gave strength to my convictions was my discovery that my principal was a no-gum man. I did not find this out, however, until I had been in the school two years, during which time I had outlawed gum fairly successfully. If you are going to be rigid about something, be rigid about what everyone else is rigid about. At least you are in good company. Even after I had found out the great truth about gum, however, my class was still protesting that it wasn't fair, since their teacher let them chew gum last year.

3

the insecurity games

Aw, We Did This Last Year. Every class I have taught begins the year with a dedicated mission: to enlighten their new teacher about Last Year.

According to my students, Last Year must have really been something. Last Year they were allowed complete freedom all the time, they had better art, better physical education, longer recesses, better parties, easier and more interesting work, and nobody ever got in trouble.

When you are a first-year teacher, this campaign is likely to get to you, since you have thinner skin and you haven't developed an I-couldn't-care-less-what you-did-last-year attitude. You are fresh out of student teaching. You want your students to like school and to like you, too. You want them to learn, and you want them to get excited about the lessons and activities you have planned. As a beginning teacher, I felt quite insecure when my first two art lessons (which I had planned so carefully) were greeted with, "Aw, we did this last year. But it was better, because we painted it." Granted, only two or three pint-sized crepe hangers made these tactless comments, but it only takes two or three. The rest of the class had probably forgotten about doing it last year and were thinking the art lesson was going to be pretty enjoyable. But the complainers got under my skin, and I began to think maybe there *was* a better way of doing it. Maybe I should have planned something else, maybe it was a dumb idea after all.

Children are quick to pick up a teacher's feelings, especially his feelings of insecurity. Then they close in for the kill. (When they are *not* sensitive to your feelings is when you wish they were, such as when you don't feel well and wish they would behave like Grade-A angels for a few hours!) I learned during the

21

first months of my first year not to let the complainers and the insecurity peddlers bother me or, if they bothered me, I learned to cover up successfully.

Here are some ways I handled "But we did this last year!"

1. "Good. I heard it was so much fun, I thought we'd try it again this year."

2. "Do you remember what you made? Good. This year try to make one that's completely different so you don't have two exactly alike."

3. One of my fellow teachers gave me his formula. I was asking him about all these things that his ex-students supposedly had done when they were in his class. "Oh, we did do something like that," he said, "But it was a bit different. I always answer the complainers this way. I tell them that now they're in the THIRD grade, and *so* much older, theirs will be so much better this year!" I have used this answer, too, with great success.

4. "Did you really do it last year? Well, I've never done this with my class before, and I'm really anxious to try it. And you can really help me out, since some of you already know how to do it."

Whatever you do, you can't afford to give in and say, "Oh, no. Don't you people *ever* like anything? Stop complaining and pay attention," even if you really feel that way.

A teacher has to be something of a Pollyanna and make sunshine out of every potentially bad moment. If you are positive and resourceful and can bounce back, you are likely to influence your students to be that way, also. Just think, next year, they will be telling their new teacher in September how great it was in your class. Then he can feel insecure, too.

Invoking Parental Support. This is a game played by the more socially adept child. He has probably been using the reverse of this technique at home on his parents. This child is the one who always tells his mother that Dad lets him do it. He tells his mother that he gets to do it at the babysitter's. If he's at his grandparents frequently, his mother is probably sick of hearing about what Grandma lets him do.

This game is similar to Sowing Seeds of Insecurity, but it has a somewhat different twist. In the school situation, this child tries to play you off against his parents. He tells you his mother doesn't like him to play kickball in his new boots, and if you make him do it, she will be very mad at you. This child may also state firmly that his father doesn't like him to have any homework on weekends because it interferes with family outings. This is the child who doesn't study his spelling because his mother says it is a waste of time. This child doesn't want to sit by Sandy because her mother doesn't like her to play with her.

I handle these challenges by asking the child nicely to be sure to have Mother or Father write me a note stating his requests, which I will probably grant. "I need to have it in writing, Marcy." You don't say, "Who does your father think he is? It's not up to him whether you do your homework or not. What nerve!" This undoubtedly is the way you feel, but keep it to yourself. For one thing, the child will rush home and tell his family what you said, word for word. This is very bad for your image and doesn't help community relations one bit. No, the request for a note is safer. In only one instance has a child brought me a note from home in response to my setting this condition. In this note, mother said that she didn't want Jimmy to play kickball in his new boots, and would I please tell her what days we had PE so she would be sure he wore something else? Touché, Jimmy!

If you could eavesdrop in the homes of children who attempt the Parental Support game, you would probably find that parental remarks went something along these lines:

1. The new boots weren't really supposed to be worn to school, and it is the child, not you, who will get in trouble if he ruins them.
2. Dad probably told the child that if he didn't start using his school time better, there would be an end to camping trips altogether.
3. What mother thought was a waste of time were the hours she has spent helping her reluctant son with his spelling. She never mentioned you.
4. Mother never heard of Sandy before. It's just that Patty doesn't like her.

Never fear—if a parent really has strong feelings about your standards, procedures, or actions he is likely to make it known to you or the principal by more direct means than by having his child express his dissatisfaction for him.

The "Why Me?" Technique. This ploy, and the next one—the Open Challenge—are, by far, the most difficult to handle. Fortunately, most children do not use them. They are favored by the special few who are a bit emotionally disturbed. Whenever you hear a child using the "Why Me?" technique, beware and tread softly. You may have a potential social misfit on your hands. The "Why Me?" child will tell you that teachers always pick on him. He has two strikes against him right from the start. He gets blamed for everything whether or not he was guilty. No matter how hard he tries, he always gets into trouble. He has one set of problems after another with teachers and other adults, and it is because they all hate him. He also reasons that the other kids don't like him either because they are always trying to get him into trouble.

Your first reaction to the "Why Me?" child is probably to contradict him: "Oh, no, Roger. That isn't true. What nonsense! How can you say people are always picking on you?"

This is a counterproductive approach, especially if you tell him this in public. Now Roger feels as if you are definitely not on his side. You don't understand him and, what is worse, he can now tell that pretty soon *you* are going to start picking on him, too, just like all the other teachers.

Another difficulty with contradicting Roger is that he is right, to some extent. Teachers *do* pick on him, but this is mainly because he is always doing things to annoy or bother others. He does get in trouble a lot, because he is always breaking rules. Pretty soon he gets teachers to dislike him. The way to approach this child who is probably a boy (very rarely a girl) is to level with him. Suppose Roger is doing something undesirable in class during the first week of school. Let's say he constantly talks to the child who is sitting next to him, and let's also say you suspect that what he is saying is none too complimentary towards you or the school and might be a bit rough for other fifth-graders. You have gently reminded the two talkers that they should remember your rule: "We work quietly."

Finally, after these reminders have obviously done no good, you quietly tell the two boys that you can no longer allow them to sit together, as they are disturbing the other members of the class. By this time you suspect that Roger initiates the talking. Mike, the boy he sits next to, is a good-natured soul who will go along with anything. He would probably be just as happy if Roger sat someplace else. When you inform the boys that they will have to be separated, Mike's reaction is likely to be one of relief. He probably wants to accomplish more during class than he has up until now, but Roger's seductive conversation was too hard to pass up.

Roger doesn't feel relieved, however. He feels angry. For one thing, he is fully aware that he is at fault and Mike is not. He sees that Mike is being punished, too, and he probably realizes that if he weren't sitting by Mike, Mike wouldn't have gotten in trouble for talking in class. So Roger feels just a little guilty. And we know how people deal with guilt feelings, don't we? Right! They rationalize and lash out against other people. Roger lashes out against you (when he is really angry with himself), and he rationalizes his guilty actions by blaming you.

"Teachers are always picking on me," he grumbles as you help him move his seat. "That's not fair. I always get in trouble for nothing."

So you ask Roger to sit down quietly in his new seat and suggest that he talk with you at the next recess, or take him outside the door out of earshot of the rest of the class. When you and he are alone you tell him, "You know, Roger, school has just started, and I don't know you very well. You don't know me very well, either, do you?"

Roger will nod in agreement. He doesn't know what to expect.

"Even though I don't know you very well, I can tell you that I am going to like you. But sometimes people you like do things that you don't like. Right, Roger?"

"I guess so," he will reply.

"So even though you may sometimes do things that I don't like, I will always like *you*. See what I mean?"

Cut it short and send Roger back in to sit in his new seat. He will probably not give you any trouble for a little while because you have given him some food for thought. You will probably need to remind this child often that it is not *he* you are displeased with, it is *what he did*. Try to chide him with a smile and, maybe, a slightly jocular touch.

"Oh, great, Roger, I'm sorry you will have to stay in just a while after school. I wish you hadn't talked so much in line, so I wouldn't have to do this. We love to listen to you, but some other time, okay?"

If you are smiling, Roger can't help but feel a little better about staying after school. After all, you didn't say, "Roger Jones. That is the last time I am going to speak to you about your constant talking in line. You are always bothering people. Stay after school."

When I hear words like those, I visualize an old lady school-teacher with a pince-nez and service oxfords. The unfortunate thing is that I have heard the same kind of remarks from the lips of young, tuned-in teachers who should have known better.

You must also remember to praise Roger when he does something right. Keep your praise adult and nonsaccharine. Roger is not one to be won over by sweet words. Set up situations for Roger to do good deeds and have successes. Choose him occasionally to get a book you need from the library. Let him take messages to the office. Let him run other errands. Thank him each time and tell him he did a good job, that you really appreciated it.

The Open Challenge. The Open Challenge is a technique that you will encounter very seldom in most classes. It is frightening when it occurs, and it is fortunate that it does not happen very often. The child who chooses to challenge you directly is usually one of two types: he is either a child who falls in the general category of "emotionally handicapped," or he is a sullen, perennial misbehaver. Ordinarily you will have one or two children of this type in your classroom each year.

The majority of children in the regular classroom do not deliver Open Challenges to their teachers. They do not need to.

The Open Challenge usually gets a child in a great deal of trouble, and will not be used by one who is reasonably well-balanced. Although many children resent adult-teacher-school authority to some extent, most are not hostile and resentful. A child may challenge you out of sheer nastiness, or he may temporarily lose control of his better judgment. He may also be testing you, but it is more likely that the normal child will test you in the other ways that I have discussed.

If you have been reasonably lucky in your student teaching, you have probably not been challenged. A good master teacher will try to set up student teaching experience so that it will run smoothly without confrontation with severe behavior problems. I have mixed feelings on this count. I agree with the master teachers who do this, because there is no way that a student teacher can command the authority of the regular classroom teacher who has had the advantage of knowing his pupils and how to handle them since the beginning of the year. No matter how skillfully a student teacher handles a challenge delivered by one of his charges, he and the pupils both know he is not "their" teacher. On the other hand, a protective attitude on the part of a master teacher does not give a student teacher a chance to learn how to handle the crisis situations that inevitably arise even in the best-managed classrooms.

An Open Challenge is sometimes called "open defiance." This may occur when a child flatly refuses to do something you have asked him to do. His attitude is usually, "Just try and make me do it." In general, I follow the practice of never answering a challenge by laying down an ultimatum. Never back an angry child or yourself into a corner. You will both say and do things you will later regret. Here is how I handled my first Open Challenger.

The challenge was made in my very first day of teaching. I noticed, as my students and I were checking each other out, that one boy stood out as a potential troublemaker. The rest of the children were pretty good. But not Manuel. He had tested me all morning in the milder ways I have already mentioned. By lunch time, he was ready to escalate, and I was ready to quit my job. It is surprising how the behavior of one child can upset one so much.

After lunch, I began to read the children a story that I had carefully selected. It was a charming story about a child and her pet hippo. I began to read feeling quite confident. Oral interpretation of literature is one of my talents, I reminded myself. My voice was no longer quavering as it had been during the first half hour of the morning.

After the first few minutes, I noticed that Manuel was slumped down in his chair (the largest in the room, but still too small for an 11-year-old young man in the fourth grade) with a look of utter disgust on his face. He obviously thought the story was a big old drag. The other students who were in the 8-to-10-year-old age bracket were very interested and amused by the adventures of Hippy Hippo and Alice, his owner. Manuel began to make noises halfway between groans of displeasure and gastric distress. The smirk on his face made it clear that it was not his lunch that was disagreeing with him. He began to make loud sucking noises on his arm. He rattled his ruler inside his desk. Most of the class was now paying more attention to Manuel than to me.

I began desperately to look for something that would stop these distractions. I remembered from my student teaching experience that I had often quelled distraction by stopping talking or reading. This had always worked, so now I stopped reading and looked up from the book. Three children in the front of the room noticed that the teacher wasn't reading any more, but the rest were attending to Manuel. Finally I said in a friendly voice, "Manuel, we're waiting for you so we can finish the story."

He stopped his antics. This will hold him, I thought. Score one for the teacher. It lasted about five seconds. Manuel was now singing to himself and drumming his fingers in his desk to keep time. In the bad old days, the mighty teacher would have risen up in righteous wrath and slammed a ruler down across Manuel's knuckles and sent him to the principal's office. I knew these options were not open to me, and I also knew that there were better ways of handling behavior problems. But what? It was obvious that I had to stop Manuel, or forever lose esteem in the eyes of the other youngsters. I envisioned them blabbing it all to their parents that night at supper. "Manuel was being bad, and the teacher didn't even *do anything*! She doesn't care what you do in class!"

Manuel sang on, and now the rest of the class were looking at me. Many were giggling, I think, out of embarrassment for me. No child really likes to see his teacher humiliated. Instinct and maybe even good common sense told me I had to isolate Manuel from the reinforcing attention he was receiving. The more the other children noticed him, the more enthusiastically he would "entertain" them with his misbehavior.

"Boy, this is dumb. I don't want to listen to this stupid story no more." remarked Manuel.

I stood up quietly, closed the book, walked over to Manuel's desk, and said, "Manuel, please come outside." I did not attempt to chastise or threaten him in front of his peers. My remarks were for his ears only. Quickly I escorted him outside, and I stood face to face with this sullen young man who was almost as tall as my five feet three inches.

"Manuel, I am sorry you do not like the story. It seems to me that the rest of the class was enjoying it. I cannot tolerate your distracting behavior in our classroom. When we go back into the classroom, you will sit quietly in your seat, and I will finish the story without any further disturbances on your part. Is this clear? If you behave in this manner again, I will be forced to discuss it with the principal and your parents."

Manuel saw the loophole and grabbed at it.

"My parents don't understand English," he said.

"That's no problem," I said confidently, "there are plenty of people at our school who speak Spanish. They would be glad to help us explain what you have been doing. I am sure your parents will understand exactly what you have done."

I called his bluff. I had no trouble with Manuel for the rest of the day. He was contrite later at recess when I had him sign a formal pledge, promising to try and do his best in upholding the conduct standards of our room. I promised him that the incident would be forgotten as long as no further misbehavior of its kind occurred. If it did, the pledge he had signed would be made available to the principal and his parents, with the help of an interpreter. Not only would he be accountable for misbehavior, but he would have broken a solemn promise.

After this first encounter, I have had to deal with a few Manuels, and I have used basically the same technique. When I thought the matter over during the next few weeks of school, during which Manuel was tractable and pleasant, if not angelic, I discovered that there were many psychological advantages to the approach I had used. In the first place, I had not backed Manuel into a corner, nor did I humiliate him in front of his peers. I didn't become panicky and shout at him: "If you don't stop that right this instant, I will make you go to the office."

This would have forced Manuel to keep it up, so I would have to make good my threat. It would have also shown the children and the principal that this teacher was a flop at handling discipline problems. Sending Manuel to the office on the first day of school would have been a disaster. The principal would not have been available to see the child, so he would have sat in the office having a high old time. He also would have escaped hearing the rest of the story, which is exactly what he wanted. I made it necessary for him to listen to it on my terms. I believe that I presented myself to Manuel as a teacher who wasn't going to be manipulated by him, but one who hadn't commited herself to disliking him. I think he saw me as being reasonable. I only demanded from him what I knew he could give—nothing more or less than the other children were asked to do. When I discussed the matter with him at that next recess, I pointed out that listening quietly to a story, even one that he disliked, wasn't such a terribly difficult thing to do. "I know you can do this," I said.

As you may have guessed, Manuel was a great help to me all year, and he even returned the following year before school to help me get my room ready for next group of fourth graders.

At the end of the year, his mother told me (as translated by Manuel's elder sister) that I had been Manuel's favorite teacher, and that he talked about me a lot at home. This affection was more than I really hoped for at the beginning of the year. I only wanted his obedience and wasn't asking for his affection. Perhaps by insisting on the former, the latter followed naturally.

Even if Manuel hadn't liked me later on, I think he would still have behaved himself. But a little affection goes a long way!

Here is another example of an Open Challenge. Kathy was a child who had many learning problems, most of them of an emotional origin. She was quite immature, compared to most of the other fourth-grade girls, even though she was ten going on eleven. She had difficulty getting along with both boys and girls, and was always running to me to solve her many problems in relating to her classmates. She was quite dependent on her mother and on me.

Kathy's learning problems were aggravated by the fact that she was reading at about the low-second-grade level. She was receiving special help from the school district's reading specialist, who conducted a 40-minute remedial clinic every day for Kathy and four other girls with reading problems. The other girls each wanted to be "the best," and competed strenuously with one another for the honor. This competitive atmosphere only intensified Kathy's dislike of reading.

On the day in question, nothing had gone well for Kathy. I had been trying to help her with her work, with mutually frustrating results. She had not responded to my efforts and paid little attention to me or to her work. Although I tried to be patient, I began to feel irritated, and I am afraid my feelings were beginning to show.

Finally I said, "Kathy, you must try a little harder. I want you to do better in reading, but if you aren't trying your best, we can't make progress. You would like to read better, wouldn't you?"

Most poor readers respond to this question very positively. They always say yes, they would like to be better readers, and then they redouble their efforts and forge ahead. Children with reading problems need a great deal of reassurance, and they easily become discouraged. Things that are easy for the other children are difficult for them, and they feel stupid at not being able to cope. I attempt to reassure them by pointing out that they *do* have control over their destinies.

"Come on," I say, "we can do it together. Let's dig in and go places!"

Although such exhortation may seem banal and trite, it often provides the push needed to get children to work on their reading problems.

On this occasion, Kathy did not respond favorably to this approach at all. Instead, she said: "I hate reading, and I don't care if I learn to read. Everybody tries to make me read, and I won't."

I replied, "Kathy, I'm sorry you dislike reading. However, reading is very important, and it's something you will be doing lots of in school. If you could learn to like it a little better, then I think you might begin to read better."

She shook her head sullenly. Defeated, I sent Kathy back to her seat. She was feeling very angry at the world and began to annoy the children sitting by her, who were working on their own reading work. The girl who sat next to Kathy was drawing a picture to go with a book she had just finished reading. Kathy reached over and snatched one of the girl's crayons.

"Give it back, Kathy," snapped Vicky, the other girl.

Kathy responded by throwing the crayon on the floor. Vicky gave her a push and demanded that she pick it up.

At that moment, I was having a reading conference with Todd, who was very excited about a book he had just read on Daniel Boone. He had launched into an enthusiastic discussion of Boone's boyhood, and I hated to be interrupted. Todd treasured his time alone with me, and resented interruptions.

I reluctantly told the boy to wait a minute and said, "Kathy, please try to work more quietly. Todd and I are having a conference."

Kathy ignored me and began to hide Vicky's crayons in her desk. By this time, other children had gotten involved.

"Cut it out, Kathy. We're trying to work." they said. "You took Vicky's crayons, Kathy. I saw you!"

I sent a disgruntled Todd back to his seat, promising to finish his conference later, and went over to Kathy's desk to ask her what was happening. Her "helpful" seatmates began to set the teacher straight.

"Oh, Mrs. Fisk," said one boy, "Kathy was taking Vicky's crayons and hiding them in her desk."

"I was not," snapped Kathy.

"Yea," said another boy, hoping to climb on the bandwagon of Kathy's destruction, "and she knocked my book on the floor, too."

"Now, wait a minute," I said, ignoring the second accusation, "Kathy, did you take Vicky's crayons?"

"No!" replied Kathy in a nasty tone.

"You are lying, Kathy," said the first boy.

"Well," I said "Vicky, why don't you get the can of crayons from the closet and use those until your own crayons show up?"

It was almost ten o'clock, and Kathy was scheduled to go the reading specialist then. My hope was to stall for time and get her out of the room without further incident. When she was gone, we could search her desk for Vicky's crayons, and I could ask Vicky to let the matter drop. Vicky graciously consented to using the extra crayons from the coffee can.

I went back to my desk, foolishly assuming that all was well and that Kathy would keep out of trouble for the next five minutes. With high hopes, I asked Todd to bring his book and his chair back to my desk so that we could finish his conference, but no such luck. Kathy began jostling Vicky's arm while she drew. Vicky, however, showed considerable empathy and self-control, because she picked up the coffee can and her drawing paper and moved to the "quiet corner" in the back of the classroom. She could see which way the wind was blowing with Kathy. Kathy put her head down on the desk.

"Kathy's sleeping in class," said one of her tormentors.

Todd was holding forth on Daniel Boone again. I glanced at the clock. "It's time for you to leave now, Maria," I said to one of of the other girls who went to the reading specialist with Kathy. "Get Kathy and go before you're late."

"No," said Kathy. "I'm not going."

"Mrs. Fisk," called Maria, with a note of malice in her voice, "Kathy says she won't go!"

At that, everyone on Kathy's side of the room looked up. "Oh, boy," they thought, "Now let's see what the teacher does."

Todd gave me a baleful look, and dragged his chair back to his desk. Just as with Manuel, I now had the unasked for and unwanted attention of everyone in the class. It had been a year and a half since Manuel, and I had not received an Open Challenge in the meantime.

Once again, I attempted to break the larger problem into bite-sized morsels. I sent Maria on the reading specialist alone, and asked her to tell the specialist that Kathy would be along shortly. This may have been a mistake on my part, because it gave Kathy time to decide that she wasn't going—no matter what.

"Kathy," I said, after Maria had left, "it's time to leave now."

"I won't go!" she shouted. "I'm never going to go again."

Challenge delivered.

We'll see about that, I thought. In retrospect, the best thing to do would have been to tell Kathy that she didn't have to go today, and get her set up with crayons and paper in the back of the room while the rest of the class had their language lesson. Then I could have talked to her later and discussed the problem with the reading specialist at lunch time. But I didn't do it that way and, instead, tried the approach I had used with Manuel. I asked Kathy to step outside, and she came dragging her heels. Once out of the room, I told her, "Kathy, I'm afraid that you have to go to reading today. Mrs. Schultz is expecting you, and you must go. Please do as I ask. Please start walking, and we'll talk about this later."

Kathy did indeed start walking, as I requested, but she never arrived. The phone buzzed 10 minutes later while we were writing stories about Abraham Lincoln. It was the school office, wondering why Kathy Jacobsen had not shown up for her reading session.

"I sent her ten minutes ago," I replied.

The secretary reported that one of the other girls (Maria, undoubtedly) had said that Kathy was probably hiding in the girls' rest room. I replied that I would appreciate it if they would look for Kathy and keep her in the office until recess. I didn't want to send one of my students to look for her, because I felt it was better that they didn't get any more involved in this situation. They would tease and torment Kathy for days. Besides, I really didn't want them to know that Kathy had disobeyed me and had not gone to the reading specialist as I had directed.

I hung up and saw one of the boys who was our resident busybody raising his hand. Although I was certain that he didn't need any help, I walked over to his desk, and asked, "What can I do for you?"

"Is Kathy in trouble?" he asked, maliciously.

"Jon," I said as pleasantly as possible, "Why don't you concentrate on writing your story. Don't worry about other people's problems."

The office called back to say that search of the girls' rest rooms had not produced the wayward Kathy, but that she had been found hiding in the bushes near the door to the reading specialist's room. The reading specialist had taken her to the office, finding her too defiant and upset to stay in the reading group.

At recess, I went to the office and talked to Kathy who by then had spent 20 minutes cooling off. She had been crying. She felt badly about all the trouble she had caused and was very sorry that she had made me angry. I told her that I regretted having to speak harshly to her and expressed the hope that it wouldn't happen again, as well as the expectation that she would go to the reading specialist without any further problems. I also told her I was sorry that she felt the way she did about reading, but that Mrs. Schultz and I wanted very much to help her. I tried to convey the impression that we would continue to try to help her, whether she cooperated or not.

Kathy was quite contrite, and apologized profusely. She even apologized for having spoiled Todd's conference, and wondered if she should write him a note saying that she was sorry. I said that wasn't necessary, that he would forgive her anyway. "He'll have his conference tomorrow," I said. She also said she would try harder in reading.

Kathy held my hand on the way back to the classroom. Upon seeing a tearful and solemn Kathy walking with the teacher on the way back from the office, the rest of the class assumed that she had met stern punishment at the hands of their teacher and, maybe, even the principal. They were reassured that Kathy had been dealt with properly, and their confidence in me was restored.

Kathy went to reading every day from then on with no complaints. She occasionally indulged in a little fooling around once she arrived there, but our very understanding reading specialist was able to handle this capably. Kathy never defied me or the reading specialist after this, although she continued to have many problems with reading and the other children.

There are no rules for dealing with a specific type of Open Challenge; every case is different, and the teacher often has to "play it by ear." In general, however, it is safer to adopt the "friendly but firm" approach, as I did with both Manuel and Kathy. The advantage of this tack is that you can maintain enough detachment to observe what is going on within the child, as well as between the child and the other actors in the situation, including yourself.

Some teachers believe that they are justified in showing their anger when they meet with an Open Challenge, saying that this imparts a note of genuineness to the situation, and that children just cannot believe in adults who never get angry. My answer to this is that anger is a two-edged sword that can be very devastating in the hands of a teacher. The teacher is always in a "power relationship" with children and, as a result, has to be extremely careful about the effect she is having on them. It is control through respect she wants, not control through fear. I won't claim that I have never lost my temper in the classroom, but in looking back on the incidents, it has seemed to me that things would have worked out better if I hadn't done so. It is important at such times to keep the losses at a minimum. I can say that I have lost some Open Challenges, but I have not lost the class. And losing one Open Challenge with a child does not mean that you cannot win the next one. Manuel and Kathy are among my successes, but note that they won the early skirmishes.

If the teacher can remain objective in the face of an Open Challenge, she will realize that she always has a number of alternatives facing her. As she takes each step in the encounter with the disturbed and disturbing child, she must consider where her alternatives are leading her and what her resources are. It is no disgrace to fail when confronted by an Open Challenge: Open Challengers are likely to be quite skillful in getting adults to lose their temper or back down.

One thing I have done when I feel myself getting angry is to tell the child just that—that I am getting angry and may lose my temper, so don't push me any further. In many instances this was enough to bring the child up short and to survey what he was doing.

4

routine misbehavior, misdemeanors, and assorted minor crimes

The list of Games Children Play with their teacher is literally endless, but there are certain forms that recur time and time again. Individually, they are unimportant, but as one after another are played during the school day and throughout the week, they have a cumulative effect that is exasperating and draining. Here are some of the most popular games.

Inappropriate chatter. If a child seems to have difficulty controlling his talking during class, it is probably the result of the company he keeps. Try moving his seat away from the child who is helping him indulge in such mutually enjoyable, although distracting, conversation. Place him next to someone with whom he is not particularly friendly (but not someone he violently dislikes, because this can cause arguments) or a child who has proven himself to be an industrious worker who is not easily distracted. If the talking continues with each new partner, you may be doing this child a service by letting him sit apart from the group. Move his desk completely out of the line of fire. If he is an undauntable chatterbox, perhaps a dose of behavior modification (see Chapter 6) may be what the doctor ordered.

Fidgeting and fiddling. If this child is not keeping any contraband toys in his desk, but is playing with school supplies and writing implements, it may be that he needs a change of pace. He may be an immature child who has difficulty concentrating for the duration of the lessons or activities at your grade level. Try getting him to turn his chair around to face you squarely when you are instructing him, thus preventing hands from wandering into his desk at all. Stand closer to him than you have been doing, and see if this doesn't help cut down on fidgeting.

If the problem is really chronic, and if the child is also very tense, perhaps you need to get the school psychologist into your room to observe him. It is possible that he is hyperactive and, for some neurological reason, cannot control his urge to squirm or fidget. Make sure this child cleans out his desk often, to avoid a buildup of interesting clutter, and keep him occupied with small, short tasks.

Arguing. Judging from what we know about American families today, arguing and bickering seem to be a way of life for many. With such solid training in the home, it is no wonder that many children will start or participate in an argument at the drop of a hat. There isn't a great deal you can do to abate this tendency, but you can be prepared to step in and dampen the tension whenever you sense that a dispute is brewing.

Private talks with children who argue frequently may help a little. Many arguments start over the most ridiculous things, and if you can get the participants to see the humor in the situation, you've come a long way. I find that if two children habitually argue, the best advice you can give them is to suggest that they avoid each other. Some experts would be horrified at this approach, saying that a teacher should help these youngsters to learn to accept each other and to work out their communication problems whenever they occur. This may be true, but it is definitely more practical to teach children to walk away from situations before the anger boils over. Most adults realize that if they are annoyed with their fellow workers or their spouses, and are on the verge of having unpleasant words with them, the best thing to do is to leave the scene until the hostility dissipates somewhat.

Pinching, pushing, grabbing, and other sleight-of-hand tricks. Some children are very aggressive physically and seem to have great difficulty in controlling their impulses. It is indeed a sorry fact that many never outgrow this annoying tendency and as immature adults, can be seen every day behind the wheels of cars on the streets and highways, running red lights, cutting in, tailgating, and the like.

You can avoid a lot of this antisocial behavior in the classroom by being methodical and orderly about such things as having the children line up for visits to the library or for recess. As a beginning teacher, I was very careful in the way I had my children line up to go outside for play, but I was foolish enough to believe that such painstaking training would carry over into other situations in which large numbers of children needed to stand close together. The first time my class was to go next door to see a film I said, "Please pick up your chairs, boys and girls, and line up at the back of the room." The horrifying, tumultuous crush that resulted from my folly was enough to teach me the error of my ways.

Ordering the children back to their seats, I tried another approach.

"Will all the girls on the right side of the room please stand."

They stood.

"Will you girls now pick up your chairs and stay where you are."

"Now, you girls may walk slowly to the back of the room and form a straight, single-file line without touching anybody or any furniture. Let's see what a good job you can do."

Mission accomplished, I then repeated the same series of instructions for the boys on the left side of the room, the girls on the left, and the boys on the right, until everyone had was standing in a straight, silent line at the back door. Then, and only then, did we walk next door.

This divide-and-conquer method can be used successfully in situations when you want children to view something that is stationary, like a visitor's pet parrot or a child's foreign stamp collection. You can have them parade by the display one by one, returning immediately to their seats. Don't, for heaven's sake, say, "Come take a closer look at Mr. Valdez's parrot," or you will surely have one ruffled and crushed parrot and one distraught Mr. Valdez.

If you still have problems with children who can't control their urges to grab and push, despite your precautions, try placing such children at the head of the line or away from the group at large, just as if they had problems with talking. This cuts down on the opportunity to make physical contact with other children.

"But I Was Only Borrowing It," or Petty Theft. Grand larceny, such as lifting $50 from the teacher's purse, will be dealt with under Extraordinary Misbehavior. Here, we are concerned with misdemeanors only. Many children feel that they should have unlimited access to their classmates' supplies, regardless of whether the items in question are furnished by the school or brought from home. If the item is attractive and unusual, like a W.C. Frito eraser or set of watercolor pens, everyone who sits near the owner of such a treasure assumes part ownership.

This assumption naturally proves quite irritating to the child who spent his allowance on the cute dog eraser with plastic rattling eyes, and he never intended to see it worn away into oblivion by the children who sit at his table, many of whom he doesn't especially like. He may announce loudly that nobody gets to use the eraser without permission from him, but this will not stop the pint-sized kleptomaniac (PSK). As soon as the owner of the dog eraser leaves his desk for one instant, the PSK pounces on the eraser, uses it briefly, and then drops it absent-mindedly into the back of his own desk. Often, the owner does not notice the absence of his eraser until, shall we say, during the following day's spelling test.

"Somebody stole my Rover!" (Children under the age of 11 often name many of their inanimate possessions, especially erasers) "Who took my eraser?"

Of course, you will have to start a search, with luck, after the spelling test, if you can stave off the child till then. You can make the children who sit near Rover's owner to look in their desks very carefully to see if perhaps, the eraser got in there by mistake. This gives the PSK who snatched the eraser a graceful out. He can always say that he doesn't know how it got there. Frequently the PSK will say, when the eraser is found lurking in the bowels of his desk, "But you said I could borrow it!"

Stop the argument now, return Rover, and get on with something else, or else you can settle back for a good 15 minutes of "No, I didn't," "Yes, you did," "No, I didn't."

Most petty theft in the classroom occurs when somebody (often you) lends something and the borrower genuinely does forget to return it. Or maybe he hoped you would forget you lent it to him. At desk-cleaning time, all kinds of my own personal school supplies come back to me in basketfuls, including my favorite fountain pen and jewelry that I let a child wear "Just for a few minutes."

Late Work or, "I Didn't Have Time to Finish, Teacher, Because We Went Piranha-Hunting in the Amazon Last Night." It is usually the same few children who continue to turn in their assignments late or not at all. The rest of the class is pretty punctual, with occasional slips due to illness or last-minute visits from relatives. If a child has problems getting his work done, enlist the aid of his parents. If a girl's life is crowded with many after-school activities and lessons, perhaps her family needs to help her set up a schedule so that she can squeeze her homework in between ballet and the Girl Scouts. If a child has learning problems and is having difficulty completing work for this reason, give him shorter and less-complex assignments and allow him plenty of time during class when he can do the work with your help. If I were teaching in an inner-city school, I would avoid homework as much as possible, since many students live in small, cramped apartments where they have no place to work on school assignments without noise and interruptions. In middle-class schools, however, where home conditions are more conducive to homework, completing assignments on time is a problem that most parents are willing to help you solve.

Handling Extraordinary Misbehavior. When you are faced with extraordinary misbehavior, you will surely know it. This category includes such behavior as fighting with intent to do real bodily harm; premeditated, gross disobedience; flagrant violation of important classroom rules; screaming and temper tantrums; and assaulting a school employee. Most teachers would include the loud and continual use of profane or obscene language as part of this list, but my friends tell me that in some inner-city situations, this is not uncommon and is tolerated. From what other teachers tell me, however, loud profanity and obscene language are unacceptable in most elementary schools. They are, furthermore, likely to be associated with other severe forms of misbehavior. Children, like adults, are

inclined to be consistent in their behavior. It is extremely unlikely that your best speller or your mature, poised committee-
chairman will be found shouting four-letter words in angry
exchange with you or other teachers.

Extraordinary misbehavior can be dealt wih through behavior
modification (see Chapter 6), but it is best to try something
along the following lines first. Nevertheless, if you have reason
to believe that behavior modificaton might be helpful, consider
using it in connection with the following approach.

The first thing you should do when you encounter an instance
of serious misbehavior is to call the child's parents as soon as
possible. They have a major responsibility for their child's
behavior, and you will be doing them and yourself a service if
you let them know right away that something is amiss. Not
calling home also gives you more responsibility for the misbehavior than you may wish to have. Pigeons will come home
to roost if you keep putting it off and finally, in desperation, do
call to say that you cannot stand David's fighting any longer. At
that point, on being informed that the misbehavior had been
going on for months, the parents will say that they certainly
would have done something about it sooner if they had only
known. Perhaps they would have ignored your phone call earlier, but now they have an easy way to blame the whole thing
on your negligence. Parents are not delighted at hearing bad
news about their children, but they find it a lot easier to swallow
when they are informed immediately, rather than months later.

While you are dialing David's parents, you may begin to think
that what he did may not have been so bad after all, and feel
foolish about disturbing his parents at home because of a first
offense. Gather your wits about you and keep dialing. David's
parents may be rather annoyed with him for fighting at school,
but it is unlikely that they will be angry with you for telling them
about it. If you are wondering exactly how to conduct such a
conversation, here are some things you can say. After a few
tries at this kind of phone call, you will quickly become an old
pro and will be able to run through your speech without a
quavering voice.

You: May I speak to Mrs. Green, Please? This is David's teacher.

Mrs. G: This is Mrs. Green.

You: I'm sorry to bother you at home (she has probably put in a long day's work, just as you have), but I'm afraid David had a little problem at school today, and I thought you should know about it.

Mrs. G: What did he do now? (This is obviously not her first phone call of this type.)

You: Well, it seems that he and another child in our class had a disagreement during the last recess, and I'm afraid it ended in a fight. When the yard duty teacher arrived on the scene, it seems that David had hit the other boy in the mouth. Both boys were taken to the office, and the other child had a little first aid.

Mrs. G: David said something about that, but he didn't say anything about hitting anyone. He said he and Otis had an argument. They're always arguing.

You: Well, evidently that's how it started, but I guess it got beyond the point of no return.

Mrs. G: Well, we have always told David to stick up for himself. You know how boys are, always getting into fights.

You: We know that, and we only want David and the other boy to realize that fighting on school grounds is against the rules of the school and, for their own protection, they should try to avoid fighting or hitting while they're at school.

Mrs. G: Well, okay, what would you like me to do?

You: Maybe you or your husband could have a talk with

David, and suggest that he try to control himself on the playground, so that this kind of thing doesn't happen again at school. It's important for both boys to obey the school rules, so that they don't get into trouble.

Mrs. G: Well, I'll have my husband talk to him before he goes to bed. I hope it won't happen any more at school. Will you let me know if he does it again?

You: I certainly will, and I thank you very much for your time. David's been doing very well in math, by the way, and he's making good progress in other subjects. It's just this is one little thing.

Mrs. G: Oh, thank you for telling me. I'm glad he's doing a good job with his work. Good night, Miss Goodheart.

You: Good night, Mrs. Green.

If you read carefully between the lines of the teachers' remarks in this conversation, you will notice that the tone was kept as positive as possible. The teacher emphasized that the problem was not gravely serious, and that she was fairly confident that it wouldn't recur. She remembered that however nasty and aggressive David may be he is, after all, Mrs. Green's son, and she probably loves him. Instead of saying that David punched Otis in the mouth and made him bleed, she implied that both boys were at fault, which is usually the case in childhood fights. The teacher also made it seem as though David just needed to control his impulses a little more instead of painting him as a cruel aggressor against poor little Otis. Nor did the teacher make disparaging comments about the Green's methods of child rearing when Mrs. Green said that the boy was taught to stick up for himself. Regardless of how you personally feel about fighting as a way of solving disputes, bear in mind that many boys and even girls are raised to defend themselves with their fists. The teacher did not say that fighting was bad, period, but merely that fighting at school was wrong because it was against the rules. She ended the conversation on a positive note by reassuring the mother in a way that all was not amiss, and that the child was doing fairly well academically. This served to sweeten the pill a bit. It was evident that Mrs. Green was pleased to hear the last bit of information. The teacher has succeeded in establishing open communication with the parent and, if it becomes necessary to call her again when another fight breaks out, the teacher has her foot in the door, and it will be easier next time.

After you have called Mrs. Green (and maybe Otis' parents if he was equally culpable), keep a close watch on those two children for the next few weeks. Begin keeping an anecdotal record on both boys. An anecdotal record is a card or paper (one card for each child) on which you record briefly and objectively any incident of misbehavior in which the child comes to your notice. Be quite specific, and record the date, what happened (who hit whom and what precipitated the incident), what disciplinary action was taken, and whether or not you called the child's parents about the incident. In the case of a chronic misbehaver, you need to have a record in writing of exactly what he did. Don't trust your memory.

If serious misbehavior continues, you are going to have to involve the principal and, perhaps, have a teacher-parent-principal conference, in which case your principal needs to know what the child has done and when he did it. It is much less time-consuming for the principal if you can simply hand him the child's anecdotal record card for him to read at his convenience rather than spending 20 minutes of his and your time describing the misdeeds of this child. The principal will also need the anecdotal record to refer to when he calls the child into his office for a talk. He can merely glance down at the card and say, "Well, David, it seems that last Tuesday you pulled Dianne's hair and threw her books in a mud puddle." When it's down in black and white, David is going to have a hard time denying his deeds. If the principal has to operate without an anecdotal record he is forced to say, "Miss Goodheart tells me that you were annoying a little girl by pulling her hair and throwing her books in the mud," whereupon David can get in some uncomplimentary remarks about Miss Goodheart's always picking on him. Then the principal is forced into defensive maneuvers, so to speak, and the result may be a fruitless discussion.

The next action to take is to have a private conversation with the misbehaving child. You may wish to do this before you call his parents, saying that you intend to inform them the next time anything like this occurs. During your conversation, you can use the same approach you would employ in talking with his mother. Emphasize ways he can control himself so that he does not repeat the offense. Make certain he understands exactly what he has done wrong and which rules he has broken.

A good way to end this discussion is to ask the child, "What do you plan to do next time this situation occurs?" or, "How do you plan to handle it differently next time?" If he says he doesn't know, or tries to be funny by saying next time he will hit the child harder, just explain calmly that he will have to try much harder to find another way of handling the problem. Tell him to think it over, and you will discuss it with him at another time. I would definitely call the child's family on a second offense.

While your principal reads the anecdotal record, you might ask to see him afterward to discuss ways of handling the problem it it arises again. You might wish to talk over various punishments for the offense, and see how your principal feels about particular methods. A suitable punishment for fighting on the playground might be giving up recess. Keep the child in your classroom or have him sit on the playground isolated from his friends for a couple of days. Don't leave him in your room by himself. If you prefer not to involve your principal until things get really grim, remember that it is better to let him know ahead of time that you may be needing his services in talking to the child or his parents than to wait until you have a desperate emergency on your hands.

You might ask the child's teacher from last year how he handled the child in similar situations. If the former teacher claims that he never had any problems with this youngster, don't despair and feel like a failure. The child may have changed, or he may have made new enemies in your class. Or then again, the teacher could be trying to save face!

If none of these approaches work, it might be best to involve the school psychologist. The psychologist may want to interview the child or conduct a conference with you and the parents in order to determine the best course of action. The psychologist might recommend family counseling or private psychological help for the child. It is much better for the psychologist to make this recommendation than for you to do so.

After you have done the best that you can to help your chronic misbehaver, definitely seek assistance from your principal. He can be an excellent source of ideas for a beginning teacher, and he is familiar with many such children. He will know when he needs to step in and carry the ball.

5

teaching is more than just coping

In the foregoing chapters, I discussed some of the games that children play unconsciously or consciously, skillfully or awkwardly, in their attempt to manipulate teachers and sabotage their efforts. I also noted that if children win these games, everyone loses because no one can win the learning game unless the teacher comes out on top. Teachers must win, not so much for the sheer joy of winning (in fact, in order to win, they have to pretend that there hasn't been any game) but so they can do their main job: teaching.

YOUR ATTENTION PLEASE!

A teacher cannot help a child unless she has his attention. This is a lesson that every teacher has to learn. Many beginning teachers are so intent on what *they* have planned to do what they forge ahead with their presentations before they have their pupils' attention. Or else they lose the class's attention and sail on, blissfully unaware until it is too late. So let us wander through the wonderland of daydreamers and woolgatherers, or, "I didn't hear what you said, Miss Goodheart."

Everyone admits that teachers do a lot more talking than they should. Even the most aware teachers are guilty of the sin of running off at the mouth. Talking too much is something you will have to constantly guard against because the more you talk, the less your students are going to listen. The teacher who uses words sparingly and judiciously is the teacher whose children tune in more often. And, conversely, the teacher who blathers on and on and on will have a room full of mental dropouts. We have all been to dull lectures or had college professors who droned on endlessly as we wiggled in our seats, wrote notes, or doodled. I, for one, was always glad when my fascinating teachers ended their enthralling lectures and I could make a break for the door. Most people are relieved when a long movie is over, even if they loved it. And remember that children have to listen to you all day long, and their only opportunity to listen and talk to the other kids is at recess or in class discussions.

It is, nevertheless, both obvious and necessary that you must do a lot of talking in your classroom, and it is also essential for everyone's best interests that your students listen to you when you do so. Inattention is not a cardinal sin, nor does it fall into the category of flagrant misbehavior. When a child does not listen, however, it is frustrating both for you and the rest of the children in the class, who have to listen to a repeat of the instructions they have already heard, sometimes more than once. It is also bad for the child to develop poor listening skills and habits. Listening is crucial to learning. One school I worked for purchased a set of listening skill tapes for our grade level, in hopes of making our poor listeners into good ones and our good listeners into better ones.

Attention Readiness. One rule of good teaching is don't start until they're ready. Let's say you are meeting with one of your reading groups, to whom you plan to present a review of short "e" vowels. You announce that you will be meeting with this group now and would they please bring their pencils, and crayons? Don't be surprised if they show up with their rulers and their readers instead. Remember, this is a test of the amount of attention you are getting. But maybe your horoscope has granted you a good day, and a group of six children dedicated to the pursuit of short "e's" does show up with crayons and their pencils. No, that's not correct: *four* of the six show up. They sit down and gaze at you expectantly. You are, of course, well prepared with word cards, portable chalk board, chalk, stopwatch, or whatever you are going to need for this small-group lesson, for if you have to send students scurrying around the room to collect materials for you, you will obviously have a harder time getting their attention for the lesson at hand. But you have planned well and have the tools you need.

So you sit down with the group at this point, ready to begin. The children look at you expectantly. "Let 'er rip, teach!" one of my more outspoken children once exclaimed at this juncture, eager to get started.

But you realize that you can't "let 'er rip" quite yet. There are two empty seats. What to do about them? The children are away on a brief errand and will be back shortly. You are tempted to begin without them. After all, *most* of the group has assembled, they are ready, you are ready, and the absence of two does not seem important. It appears that they could catch the drift of things when they rejoin the group. Now perhaps one can do this kind of things with adults, but definitely not with distractible children. Hence it is best not to begin the lesson until you have the entire group present and accounted for. Otherwise, you will have go over everything you've said before the stragglers arrived and will thus lose the attention and interest of the others. So begin your lesson when everyone has arrived and is sitting quietly with crayons and pencils out of fidgeting range. Now you can "let 'er rip, teach!"

When you are teaching a large group lesson, the same rules apply, within reason, of course. In some schools, upper-grade children are shifted around for different subjects of the curriculum. This involves breaking your own class up into groups who move into other classrooms for different subjects and accepting sections of other teachers' classes into your own group for the subject you are assigned. In one such situation, I was responsible for teaching all the science and health to the entire fourth grade in groups of approximately 30 children who came to my classroom three times a week.

I learned the hard way that it was pointless to begin my lesson or experiment or instructions until every child in the group was in the room, in his seat, and tuned into me! Operating on the theory that you shouldn't keep an audience waiting, I used to begin my directions or experiment when one-third of the class was present (i.e., with the children from my class who stayed with me for science that hour). Then the group from the room around the corner would show up, and I would have to reexplain after they had disrupted the continuity of my golden words by coming in the door and taking their seats. This was repeated when the group from next door came in and took their seats. By this time, the original group was bored and very fidgety, having listened to my explanation of their ecology project three times. My tactics soon changed, as you can well imagine. Perhaps grown-ups and an occasional child can slip quietly into a room, find a seat without disturbing or discommoding anybody, and figure out what is going on but this is not true of the majority of children under 14! So it is far better to bear this fact in mind and allow for it, rather than frustrate yourself and the children by repeating yourself ad nauseam.

This is how I attacked the problem of latecomers. While my own students waited for their fellow scientists to arrive, I made a last minute check of the materials needed for my lesson. If I was going to distribute any duplicated information or instructions, I laid it out on a vacant desk or table in the front of the room. I made sure my students had the correct supplies and books out on their desks. If I was going to pass out paper or scissors, I asked a child to get them out of the cupboard. As each group appeared at the door, I greeted them there, saying, "Please take your seats quietly and be ready to listen." This was of immeasurable assistance in getting the children to their seats without any more talking or shifting around than was absolutely necessary. When both groups had come in, and had thus been escorted to their seats, I waited until I had everyone's attention and all talking had ceased and then began my lesson. If there were any laggards, I said something like this: "Could we have your attention, please, Bill? We're ready to begin now."

SUPPRESSING THE COMPETITION

Even under the best of situations, a child will get the impulse to say something to a neighbor. On the face of it, this is harmless enough but, in actuality, what occurs is that the other child feels he must reply, and the first child is compelled to reply to the reply. Before anyone is aware, you have two competitors in the game of Who Gets the Class's Attention. Furthermore, not only will those two children fail to catch your directions but the other children who are sitting near them will either be listening to them and not to you or, at any rate, they will have difficulty hearing you. Here are some ways that experienced teachers use to suppress competition from chatterers.

1. Stop talking. Stopping in midsentence or midword is particularly effective. Quickly, the rest of the class will look around to see who is causing the interruption. They will no doubt frown at the offender. This also brings the daydreamer or talker back to earth because, all of a sudden, the background noise of your voice has disappeared, and he will realize that you have stopped talking. Unless he is oblivious to social conventions or your methods, he will stop whatever he is doing.

2. Start moving around the room in the direction of the offenders. Very often, your proximity and the sound of your voice getting closer and closer will be enough to stop their conversation. If you stop right next to the desk of the child who is doing the talking, the chances are that he will stop his disruptive behavior. Notice that by stopping your own talking and pausing until the child's talking ceases, or by walking over to his desk, you have not had to say anything negative or punitive. These subtle technique will usually work better than saying in your crispest schoolmarm voice: "Mary, stop that talking immediately!"

Some teachers suggest calling on the child who is not attending to the subject at hand. This is risky and seldom effective. It is risky in that you are leaving the door wide open for this child to win his peers' approval and laughter by playing the fool. It is also dangerous because you can really embarrass a child by doing this. Embarrassing a child, in my opinion, is one of the worst things you can do. Embarrassment will lower his self-esteem and instill in him an "I-don't-care" attitude, which he adopts as a defense against teachers who embarrass him. Furthermore, by calling on a child who is whispering and giggling with a friend, you are giving him a chance to be on stage.

Let us say that you are holding forth on migratory birds. You have begun the discussion by reminding the class that large fur-bearing mammals have a method of dealing with the extreme cold and lack of food that they encounter during the winter months. "That's right, boys and girls, they go into caves or dens and sleep all winter long. Who knows the scientific name for this behavior? That's right, it is called hibernation. Now, birds do something like this in the winter, don't they? Do birds go into caves or dens to sleep all winter long?" Hands wave in the air, and you call on one eager student. "No," he says, "they don't go into caves or dens." "Okay," you reply, "you're right. So therefore they all die from exposure and starvation in the winter. Right?" Wrong, obviously, and many hands wave at you. So, you think, now I'll get Mark and John back into this discussion. No wonder they do so poorly in science, they never listen! Here goes, fellows.

"Mark", you say nicely, "do all the birds die every winter?" This certainly sounds like a foolish question to Mark who, being otherwise involved, hasn't followed the discussion until this point. He thinks for a second or two that Miss Goodheart has gone off the deep end. Then he quickly realizes that she is asking him something about what the class has been discussing or listening to for the last 10 minutes.

Inasmuch as Mark is a normal human being, he will try and save face. How will be accomplish this? Just watch.

"Sure", he chirps, "they all die. See? Like this, Awk!!"

Mark collapses on his desk making choking, gagging noises. The rest of the class bursts into peals of laughter. Good show, Mark, they snicker, you're a funny guy. Maybe if he does a really good dying act his pals will ask him to repeat it at recess, and he will continue to get reinforced. What did you accomplish by calling on Mark, the errant sinner?

1. You put him on the spot by challenging him. What you really meant by asking him that question was: Mark, I know darn well you were talking to John and didn't have the foggiest notion about what we were discussing. So I'm going to let you show your ignorance to the whole class, and we can gloat over your lack of knowledge. You knew he couldn't answer the question.

2. You gave him a chance to misbehave even more. Now he has not only committed the sin of not listening to the teacher and his classmates, but he has shown off in a very silly and hostile way to the utter delight of his peers. Remember that you are teaching children, not adults. Children, being children, are amused by childish things. If Mark had been a sophomore at the University, and his zoology professor had asked him a similar question to get his attention, it is doubtful whether his fellow the students would have reacted to his dying bird routine with anything other than embarrassment. However, since Mark is an elementary school child in a room full of other elementary school children, they think his performance is the funniest thing they have seen off the TV screen. I still feel a bit annoyed when children respond to other children's ridiculous clowning around in this manner, but I know what to expect from children.

3. You didn't make your point: "Please listen to the discussion if you are going to be able to answer questions and learn something." The point you *did* make was that if you haven't been listening, you can get out of tight spot and into the limelight by showing off. The technique that Mark used was called "wising off" by children in my school.

4. You let Mark get the best of you. Who's the winner after this encounter? Not Miss Goodheart. Mark is the man of the hour. How long do you think it's going to take before you can get the rest of the class away from Mark and back to birds. Ten minutes is a conservative guess.

Let's look at the same situation with two different offenders, Judy and Dina. They, too, are whispering and giggling while the ecology discussion is going on. However, they are "good little girls," who usually listen attentively, raise their hands eagerly and often, and write neat, lovely little reports, illustrated with neat, lovely little pictures. But for once in their young lives, they are misbehaving. In this case, stopping what you're saying or moving next to them is the technique of choice. If you *do* call on them, they would be even more embarrassed than Mark, the clown. They will be crushed if you ask, "Judy, do all the birds die every winter?"

Judy probably knows more about animals and science in general than Mark, but this doesn't help her. All she knows now is that she has done Something Bad. She was whispering to Dina, and Miss Goodheart saw her, and now she is being punished by having to answer a question. Even children who almost always know the answers get very upset when they are put on the spot. So Judy's eyes will fill with hot tears, and she will stare down at her desk, and say forlornly, "I don't know, Miss Goodheart. I wasn't listening. I'm sorry." Maybe a tear or two will plop down on Judy's science book, and you can bet you won't be hearing any laughter from the rest of the class. They are dying inside for Judy. They may even dislike her for being a "know-it-all," but they feel nothing but sympathy for her right now. Children seldom laugh or smile at a another child who is visibly upset or crying. They've been there themselves too many times. And how do *you* feel after this heartrending display? Very, very small.

Judy may make you feel even smaller by apologizing to you after class. If so, I hope you apologize, too, for making her feel so guilty that she cried. You could say, "Judy, I am very sorry I upset you so much when I called on you. I'm sure you wouldn't have known the answer if you had been listening, but I am sorry if I made you feel so bad". If you smile and put your arm around her, maybe you can salvage the rest of the day for her. One Judy I knew last year, who was a very conscientious young lady, wrote a one-liner on embarrassment for her teacher, my colleague. "Embarrassment," she wrote, "is when the teacher calls on you when you weren't listening and you don't know the answer." Right on, Judy!

THE CONSTRUCTIVE DISTRACTION

As an alternative to putting your chatty little competitor on the spot, you can also attempt to get him involved in a more constructive activity. Perhaps you are demonstrating displacement of liquids by gases. You have the various pieces of apparatus laid out in front of you and are ready to begin. *Now* is the chance to call on Mark or John or Judy or Dina. You could ask them to help you set up the equipment, or you could ask them to perform one step of the investigation. But this takes very careful handling. Don't pounce on these children and demand that they come up to the front of the classroom and make fools of themselves. You bring them back to earth, of course, but you give them time to prepare for what you have asked them to do.

You might say, "Who would like to attach the plastic bag to the rubber tube?" Ten hands wave in the air. Now you can say, "Mark, how about you?" He may point out somewhat nastily that he wasn't raising his hand, but you can then say that's all right, you'd like him to do it anyway.

"Come on Mark," you encouragingly say, "I'll help you."

Now you have accomplished your original objective, which was to get your little competitor involved in *your* game. Once he has come up and assisted with the experiment, he will be tuned in for the rest of the period.

THE ATTRACTIVE NUISANCE

Children often disobey school or classroom regulations regarding bringing toys to school, much to the chagrin of their teachers. Boys as always are more guilty of this than girls. Boys are likely to keep incredible assortments of cars, toy rockets, food, miniature astronauts, yo-yos, and squirt guns in their desks. With such irresistible temptations lurking within, their hands wander into the inner reaches of their desks and, pretty soon, out comes the toy. Once it has appeared, it will be attracting the attention of every other boy sitting in the vicinity. They, too, will want to see it, touch it, and play with it.

Some toys are forbidden by general school regulation. Where I have taught, squirt guns, yo-yos, and "click-clacks" (hard plastic balls on strings) are contraband items. I therefore confiscate these automatically whenever I see them in anyone's hands, desks, or jacket pockets. They are returned to the owner at the close of the school day, if it is his first offense, or the end of the school year, if he is a repeated offender. Since I always mention on the first day of school that these toys are absolutely forbidden at all times, no one has an excuse for bringing them to school.

As far as the other toys are concerned, I make it clear that I prefer the children to leave toy cars and other such things at home. If the children choose to bring them to school, however, they may be used only at recess. At all other times of the day, toys must remain in the desks or in the coat closet. If I see a toy out during class, or if the child's hand is inside the desk playing with it, it is confiscated under the same system as contraband toys. By the end of the year, I have a drawer full of interesting items.

Children are also reminded that toys brought to school and left in desks run the risk of being stolen. If this happens, too bad. It is a foolish waste of time conducting extensive searches for toys that really shouldn't have been brought to school in the first place. (For ways to handle stealing of other items, see the section on Extraordinary Misbehavior.) The most effective practice is to get the toy away from the child and into the far reaches of your desk as quickly as possible, before it causes any more disturbance than it already has!

Don't store confiscated toys in a closet or drawer that is readily accessible to your children, because indignant young men will remove the toy at the earliest opportunity. Keeping toys deep in your desk is best because it is pretty difficult to take something out of the teacher's desk without being quite obvious about it. If the boy is able to snatch his racing car out of the closet 15 minutes after you took it away from him, he will gain lots of status in the eyes of his classmates for outsmarting the teacher.

6

learning as a rewarding activity

IN PRAISE OF PRAISE

There is a fascinating and esoteric term that has been making the rounds in educational circles during recent years: *behavior modification*. Behavior modification (or "behavior mod," as it is known to the in-group) has been touted as a cure-all and denounced as the lowest form of brainwashing or thought control. As is so often the case, extravagant praise and vigorous denuniciations are both inappropriate. The fact is that behavior modification is a useful psychological technique that can solve some of the problems faced by teachers, but a teacher needs to master many more techniques than behavior modification if she is to attain even modest goals for herself and her children.

Behavior-modification theorists and practitioners set forth one basic premise that is crucial for any individual who wants to change another's individual's behavior. The idea is that people do things for which they are rewarded or "reinforced," to use the proper psychological term. By reinforcing certain behaviors and not reinforcing others, you can bring about literally amazing changes, not only in individual comportment but also in entire groups. Behavior modification has been used with children presenting severe symptoms of problem behavior; with wild, unruly classes; and even with nonreaders. The trick is to reward the child whenever he exhibits even the slightest indication of the positive behavior that you want to see and to ignore other behavior manifestations.

One reason this approach attracted so much attention is that it challenges the traditional method for dealing with misbehavior: punishment. Behavior modification experts believe that teachers encourage a great deal of misbehavior without realizing it, because they are preoccupied with punishing children when for doing something wrong but do nothing when the same children did something right. Children who are victims of this sort of treatment figure out the rules of the game quickly. What they learn is that the only time they receive their teacher's and classmates' undivided attention is when they are naughty. When they are good, nobody notices. Since the need for recognition is a very strong drive in every human being, it is no wonder that such children continue to misbehave since it is only then that they receive any attention. Of course, their teachers cannot understand why Johnny continues to be a nuisance, inasmuch as he was punished every time he did something wrong. Negative recognition is better than none at all. It is better to be yelled at by the teacher than to fade into the background and not be noticed at all.

Most teachers agree with this theory but wonder exactly how to put it to use. It sounds simple, but is it? Sure, they say, praise Johnny when he does the right thing so that he will be encouraged to keep it up. That sounds great. Let's break Johnny of the habit of being the class pest by Positive Reinforcement! But how and when do you do this?

PRAISE: WHO, WHAT, WHY, WHEN, AND HOW

Behavior modification and its modus operandi—praise—works very simply, because praise is the most powerful tool a teacher has for shaping, molding, and changing behavior. Praising children is the road to success—theirs and yours. It is crucial that a teacher study and cultivate the use of praise because, properly used, it can bring her nothing but good results and a deep feeling of satisfaction and accomplishment. I consider praise to be my most valuable and useful teaching technique. And here's how I do it.

Who. Every child in your class will fall under the magic spell you cast with praise. The majority of children will work for praise alone. In the elementary grades, teacher approval is extremely important to any child. He wants his teacher to like what he is doing, and he wants her to say so! By praising a child, you can keep him going in the right direction. Behavior modification experts spend a great deal of time discussing the misbehaving child and how to change his behavior. Praise plays an important part in your dealings with this type of child but remember, the chronic misbehavior is an exception. Now we are talking about the typical child in the typical class.

You can begin using this approach on the very first day of school. When my students have entered their classroom for the first time and have taken their seats, the first words out of my mouth are, "I like the way everyone came in and took their seats so quietly." Then I introduce myself and get on with the first day's business. I consciously try to establish a climate of positive praise from the start. All during the first day of school, while I explain rules and standards, I dole out praise along with it. My praising remarks are usually addressed to the class as a whole. If your students have entered the room quietly and efficiently after recess, say so! Did they get out their crayons quickly and without talking? Tell them. Otherwise, how do they know they have pleased you?

Praise individual students publicly. This serves as a prompter to the rest of the children, a reminder to get with it and follow the example of the child you have just recognized. You can often bring an entire roomful of unruly children back into line by praising the one lone child who did what you wanted everyone to do.

"I like the way Janet got out her English book so quickly," you say, smiling. Lo and behold, 29 other English books appear rapidly on 29 desk tops! (But be sure you don't single out Janet for all your praise—spread it around!)

Praise rewards all the children in your class. It is your opportunity to recognize the good behavior of a child who is usually very good. I had a student one year who was extremely quiet and withdrawn. He had few friends, and was hesitant to raise his hand in class discussions, even when he knew the answer or had something worthwhile to contribute. He was an intelligent and conscientious child, but painfully shy. When I praised him publicly by saying, "I'm glad to see David is ready for art," his face would light up. I had let him know that he was not only doing the right thing but that I was pleased with *him*.

In dealing with the child who is a behavior problem, public praise can also be a useful way of "getting through" to him. You have to be a little more subtle in your use of public praise with this child, because he is often suspicious of teachers in general, and he is especially quick to detect any phoniness. So be very careful to praise him publicly when he really is doing a good job, and be careful to tone it down just a bit. After all, you are trying to encourage this child, not insult him or alienate him.

In conclusion, who gets praised? Every child in your class. Also try saying nice and complimentary things about your colleagues with whom your boys and girls come in contact; it doesn't hurt you a bit, and it will help you achieve your goal: establishing a climate of positive feeling in your classroom.

What. What you say depends on to whom you are saying it. The actual words of praise that flow from your lips are contingent upon the particular child you are praising. Every child, like every adult, is unique and responds and reacts differently to things that are said to him. In general, you should be sincere and honest in your praise, judiciously avoiding any saccharine overtones both in your tone of voice and in the content of what you are saying.

Many teachers, especially those in the lower primary grades, use an overly sweet approach with children and sprinkle their speech liberally with "sweethearts," "darlings," and "honeys." They also tend to speak in the first person plural—we—as if they were the appointed representative of some celestial organization. They say such things as, "My goodness, children. Aren't we doing a simply wonderful job over here?" while smacking their lips.

Such sugary talk is not the exclusive property of aging maiden-lady schoolteachers who have been teaching kindergarten for decades. It is shocking to note that such twaddle sometimes comes from the mouths of younger and less-sentimental teachers. It is interesting to note that some adults use the saccharine approach with children to cover up their latent hostility toward them. When I received such treatment as a child, I always felt embarrassed and outraged, even when I was a preschooler. Children see through this approach right away and really resent it.

It is also tempting to lavish sweet words and affection on children who seem starved for attention and love. However, children who are in great need of attention and affection usually don't know how to respond to it once they get it. With such youngsters, it is better to underplay and move slowly until you win the child's trust and confidence.

I find that the best formula for delivering praise begins with the words, "I like" or, "I'm happy to see." This way, you lay it right on the line. You say directly that you are pleased when you say, "I like the way James is working." If an individual child does not respond well to the "I like" approach, you can get through to him more indirectly by saying something like, "I notice you are really concentrating on that book, Willie," or, "I see you have done five subtraction problems already."

Some variations on the "I like" theme are: "It's nice to see people working as hard as the people in this group," "You're really doing a good job on this side of the room," "I can see that these people are really trying their best," and "I'm proud of the way John is working."

You don't have to praise every single thing a child does, but you do have to praise often enough and convincingly enough to keep the good things coming. A pat on the back every so often is sufficient.

Why. Children want to know how they are doing in their efforts to please their teacher and win her approval. Being young, they need this feedback more often than adults. When a child tries his best on an assignment, he wants you to realize it without having to tell you, "I did my best, teacher." As you get to know your class during the first months of school, you will know what caliber and kind of work to expect from each child in your room. When you see a paper or piece of work that it even a little bit superior to the things this child has previously turned in, let him know that you have noticed the difference.

"Gee, Martin," you say (and try to keep the tone of incredulity out of voice—this implies that you wouldn't have believed him capable of such work), "I can tell you really worked on this story. You did a good job on it."

Sometimes a child will give you little hints when he is putting forth greater effort. Be perceptive and watch out for these. One of my less-mature (and, in all honesty, rather lazy) little boys always tipped me off when he felt he was doing something praiseworthy.

"Look, Mrs. Fisk!" He would announce, "I've written almost a page on this story" or, "Today, I am trying to write neater."

He knew and I knew that most of the time he was pretty careless. So in the instances that this boy buckled down and made an effort, I certainly praised him. I never said, "Of course you've almost written a page. I can see that perfectly well. And you misspelled several words, too."

Don't expect perfection from your students. If your standards are so high that they require near-superhuman effort to reach them, your students may give up trying altogether, or they may become tense and anxious, constantly asking, "Is this okay? Is this good?"

On the other hand, in your laudable attempt to create a tolerant and supportive classroom environment, you do not need to be a pushover and accept any old thing that the pupils turn in. Maintain high standards of quality by all means, but not any higher than the children can reach. Bear in mind, too, that your standards and expectations must differ from child to child because, for many of your students, even low-average work is the very best they can do. Conversely, a gifted or bright child can do above-average work with one hand tied behind him.

One other reason for praising and encouraging your students is that by pointing out publicly what pleases you, you give the rest of the children a model to follow. It is one thing for you to say to your class, "Please work quietly" and quite another when your words of praise point to a child or group of children who are working quietly. Then the other children can look at your example and think to themselves, "Okay. Now I see what she means by working quietly. If I do what Gary is doing, then I will be working quietly, too."

Sometimes it is helpful if you hold up one of the children's papers as an example, always ask the child's permission first, since some children get embarrassed or simply mortified if their work is shown to the class as a whole. Be sure you do not keep using the same child or group of children as examples, because this will have a negative effect. The other children will begin to resent it after you have shown them Kelly's neat and spelling paper three times in one week. "She always shows Kelly's paper," they think. You will also do Kelly a disservice by continually using her work as an example. She will be branded as "teacher's pet," and will shortly become a *persona non grata*.

If you show a child's work as a sample, try not to pick out the best paper very often. Look for an average effort. Otherwise your class will soon get the idea that you only value perfection, and that the only thing that pleases you is the best one in the whole class. Teachers who continually show off the work of the best students tend to discourage their low achievers. It is better to select a good, average paper, since this would be more within the reach of a low achiever.

When you show a child's work as an example, be sure to point out what makes it praiseworthy. Don't just say, "Please look at Felicia's nice drawing." Tell the class what is nice about it. Children need specifics. You could say instead: "Boys and girls, I'd like you to look at how well Felicia has used contrasting colors in her drawing" or, "Look at the way Melvin has used capital letters at the start of every sentence."

Be careful, also, in showing examples of art work to the whole class. If you can show two or three fairly different treatments or approaches, you are encouraging creativity instead of copying. When you show one child's painting of winter, for instance, you may end up with 15 other paintings that resemble your sample painting in every detail. This is because you didn't make it clear that Felicia's painting was indeed a fine one, but there were others that were equally good, but different from hers.

When. Children can be praised whenever they are doing a good job, regardless of whether they are in the classroom, in line, in the lunchroom, in the library, or on a field trip—anywhere as long as the praise is not going to embarrass them. Children sometimes get nervous about receiving praise from their teacher when they are around older children. In these cases, you could wait until you and your students are alone in your room, and then tell them how well they did.

In general, however, the best time to deliver your praise is during the time the desired action is taking place. You catch the child in the act, so to speak, and you reward him for his good deeds when he is doing them. Praising the child while he is in the midst of doing what you want him to do tends to encourage him to continue behaving in the manner. If you can't praise him while he is actually doing the desired action (you obviously shouldn't interrupt him in the middle of his answer or oral book report), then deliver your compliments immediately thereafter. The sooner you praise him the better, because this helps to ensure a repetition of the behavior.

It is better to praise in small doses more often, than to praise generously after a long period of time has elasped. This goes along with the fact that children desire immediate feedback. The younger the child, the more he needs feedback right away. If your class has been well behaved during their math period for example, tell them so right after the period is over. Don't wait until Friday and say, "I certainly think you people have been doing a terrific job during math this week." By waiting until Friday, you run the risk of having the good behavior fade due to lack of recognition. If they have been very good on Monday, praise them on Monday and, therefore, you are likely to see the same kind of behavior on Tuesday.

Once you have started handing out praise, it will become a habit, because you will notice more praiseworthy behavior. Pretty soon, supportive remarks will flow from your lips like honey, and we all know that you can catch more flies with honey than with vinegar!

When you compliment a child on something he has done, you are not only telling him that you like what he did but also that you like him as a person. This may bother you initially if you do not especially like the child, because it will seem insincere. An interesting thing occurs, however, when you look for and respond to positive things in an otherwise unlikable child. What happens is that the child actually becomes more likable. For his part, as he senses the positive tone, he will also come to like you more and will take pains to find ways to please you and thus get even more positive reinforcement.

HOW TO INDICATE WHAT YOU CONSIDER TO BE GOOD BEHAVIOR

Every teacher is different, and every teacher could come up with a different list when asked to define characteristics of good classroom comportment. There are many diverse approaches to the training of school children, and it is not my intention to defend or advocate any one approach. There seems to be a basic difference between teachers who are more structured and those who are less structured in their approaches to classroom control. The teacher who prefers a more structured classroom environment tends to value following directions, peace and quiet in the classroom, obeying rules, and industrious, businesslike work habits. The teacher who prefers less structure tends to opt for creativity, independent critical thinking, ability to handle a high degree of freedom, and usually is not very concerned about the noise level. Obviously, most teachers today fall somewhere in between these two approaches. Many teachers would place themselves somewhere in the middle, feeling that both approaches have their merits, depending on the situation at hand. This latter is a praiseworthy approach, if you are careful to make it clear to your youngsters which rules apply in which situations. You must be able to clarify the rules of the game in every learning situation if you are going to combine these outlooks.

My master teacher in student teaching made an interesting comment about classroom management, which I pass on to you for your consideration.

"Children will do anything you want them to do", he said, "as long as you are consistent, and as long as they know just what it is you want."

In order for the children to know what you want, you must first decide what it is that you *do* what. When I started teaching, I tended to give my students too much credit for the ability to figure out what I wanted. What was very simple and obvious to me was quite vague to them. I soon learned to be pretty explicit in my explanations of what I expected from them. As I tend to be a middle-of-the-road teacher when it comes to classroom management and control, I was faced with a more complex task than I would have had if I had been extremely pro or con.

Now, how *do* you let your pupils know what you want? Praising the behavior you like is one way, as I have said. There are other ways, too, some more subtle than others. Let's suppose that you are teaching math to your group of third-graders. There are several different ways that you may wish your students to behave, each depending on the particular technique you are using at the moment. When you are explaining a concept to the whole class, you would want complete silence, rapt attention, and every child in his seat. During working periods, when the children are busy solving the problems that you have assigned, you might permit children to leave their seats for drinks of water, sharpening pencils, or trips to the rest-room.

Maybe you are working with a small group in the back of the room while the other pupils are doing their assignments. In this situation, you could allow quiet talking among the pupils who remain in their seats, as long as their conversation pertained to math only. It is fairly easy to tell even from a distance when they are discussing monster movies or who likes whom, instead of multiplication!

Perhaps you have a math game or interest center where students can go after they have completed their daily assignments, and you want the children to move freely to the center without asking your permission first, thereby not interrupting you when you are working with another group. Or perhaps you have flash cards that certain children may use for drill with a friend, and you might allow quiet talking in this instance. So, you see how many diverse standards can be appropriate in the same room, with the same room, with the same teacher, and with the same subject. You need to let your students know what is tolerable at what times. A painstaking explanation is necessary the first time you enter a new situation and, brace yourself, it will no doubt be necessary countless other times during the year. Children need to be reminded, since most youngsters do not learn a procedure or set of rules the first or even the second time. Children are also very forgetful and, as I have already pointed out in Chapter 1, even if they really do remember what you've said, they will always try to test you to see if you really meant it!

Here's the kind of thing I say about these situations during math.

"Boys and girls, when I am explaining something to everyone in the class, it is very important that everybody follow these rules. First of all, everyone will have to pay attention very closely so that you will understand how to do the problems. Secondly, everybody has to stay in his seat when I am talking, so you don't disturb anyone." (Keep clarifying and get specific.) "That means nobody may get a drink, sharpen his pencil, or leave for the restroom (unless it is a great emergency) when we are having a lesson. After I have finished explaining the work, and you are doing the assignment, you may take care of drinks and pencil sharpening."

But that's not quite good enough, because a few minutes later as soon as you have finished expounding on addition with carrying, 10 children will naturally rush pell-mell to the drinking fountain or the pencil sharpener, pushing, shoving, and arguing. To you, as an adult, such behavior is inexcusable. At recess in the teacher's room, you and your colleagues do not knock each other down in your mad rush to the coffee pot. You probably would, however, if you were all under 12! Hence, further clarification once again is necessary.

"Remember that only one person may leave his seat at a time to use the pencil sharpener or the drinking fountain. You must wait until someone sits down in his seat before you can leave your seat to take care of these things."

If, after this admonishing speech, somebody does rush to the pencil sharpener when another child is already there, simply remind him of the rules. You don't bark at the offender, just say,

"Sherry, I think you forget that you must wait until Tracey sits down before you can get up to sharpen your pencil." You may have to remind Sherry on several occasions but, eventually, she will catch on. The first time she may be testing you to see if you really meant what you said. The second time might be due to a lapse of memory.

I can see the strained looks on the faces of many idealistic and forward-thinking neophytes who have just read the above paragraph. They must think, as I once did, "Good grief. What is this woman's problem? She must have some weird hang-up about pencil sharpeners and drinking fountains. Her classroom must be like the Marine Corps. I won't make such silly rules. Let's give the kids credit for having a little sense and intelligence."

I plead innocent. My only hang-up about pencil sharpeners and drinking fountains is that their unregulated use is distracting and keeps me from doing my job properly. Wait until the fifth child has noisily ground his pencil in the sharpener during a 15 minute explanation of carrying when multiplying two-place numbers. In the end, everyone listens to the pencil sharpener instead of your lesson. Freedom is a fine thing for children, as long as they do not infringe on the rights of others. A child usually does not realize when he is violating other people's rights and, as sensitive and aware as many children are, the average child doesn't see that by sharpening his pencil when you are giving a lesson, he is preventing the rest of the class from learning. Freedom is certainly not curtailed completely. I do not forbid my children to use the pencil sharpener or get a drink of water. They *do* have the opportunity to exercise this freedom at other times, so they are not deprived of it. And lastly, certainly give the children credit for having a little sense and intelligence. They had enough intelligence to see the loophole in your directions about using the pencil sharpener and the drinking fountain, didn't they? They knew you didn't stipulate how many of them could use it at one time. They demonstrated this capacity for critical thinking by charging up to the pencil sharpener en masse.

A subtle way of eliciting the behavior that you desire is ignoring the undesired behavior until the child in question adopts the correct way of behaving. A case that comes to mind is Michele, a child in one of my science classes. I had made it clear to the children that they were to remain seated and raise their hands in the event that they needed assistance from me. I made this rule to prevent little parades of children from following me all over the room as I move around giving help. Michele never quite believed me on this score, and whenever she wanted help, which was very often, she would hop out of her chair and rush up to me. If I was walking toward another child who had complied by raising his hand, Michele would trot along behind me like a puppy. Sometimes she would wait to make her request until I had finished talking to the other child, but she would often cut in on my conversation. Both of these behaviors annoyed me very much, and I set out to straighten Michele out. It took almost three months of concerted effort, but I finally had Michele raising her hand like the rest of the children. Whenever Michele would leave her seat and begin following me, I pretended that she wasn't there—no easy job! If she started asking her question, I would turn my back and walk away. If I happened to be facing her, thus giving her the impression that she had my attention, I would stare right through her. Finally she would return to her seat in frustration.

I realized that my seemingly rude actions were very hard on Michele, but I also realized that if I allowed her to continue in this manner, it would not be long before other children would decide that there was no point in staying in their seats if they could get just as good service by following me around the room when they needed some help. They would figure if she could get away with breaking the rules, they could too. When Michele would raise her hand after having no success with stalking me down, I would quickly go to her desk with a friendly smile, prepared to give her the help she wanted. When I would arrive at her side, I would say, "Michele, I am glad you remembered to raise your hand," or, "I am happy to answer your question because you remembered to stay in your seat until I came."

In this way, Michele saw that there was a method in my madness and that the reason I was ignoring her when she left her seat to find me was that she was approaching me in the wrong manner.

7

teaching as a subversive activity

TO BRIBE OR NOT TO BRIBE

The use of the Tangible Reward (read "bribe") is frowned on by some people, who maintain that children will learn only when they undertake something for highly personal reasons (intrinsic reward), and that any kind of payoff (extrinsic reward) interferes with learning and makes children dependent on the reward giver. My reaction to this position is that all human behavior, particularly learning, operates on some kind of a payoff or reward basis. In the final analysis, the most significant rewards are the personal, intrinisic ones, and this is what some of my teacher friends have in mind when they frown on extrinisic rewards. With young learners, however, the intrinisic rewards inherent in learning to add up a column of figures without an error are seldom obvious, and we must therefore "arrange matters" so that they find learning to add more satisfying than not possessing this intricate skill. Indeed, a great deal of what teachers do consists of this business of "arranging matters." The end result of the whole process *must* be satisfying and rewarding or children just will not play the learning game, to everyone's detriment. Praise is a reward, and so is the feeling of being in a busy, successful group of learners.

What is slightingly called a "bribe" is, in learning situations, merely a more tangible reward. In many instances, tangible rewards have more of an impact and are more effective than symbolic rewards, like praise or teacher's marks and, as a consequence, are more useful. Behavior modification experts, for instance, use M&M candies with small children; with older children, they use for more significant rewards like toys, trips to the zoo, or permission to help teachers supervise in the kindergarten playground.

Behavior-mod experts talk of "positive reinforcers'," but I prefer to call these tangible rewards "bribes," because it makes them sound more interesting or even slightly subversive. Call them what you will, everyone uses them in some way or other. And think of how many of life's pleasant outcomes come under the heading of tangible rewards: flowers and candy to one's hostess, testimonial dinners, wedding gifts, and even end-of-the-month paychecks!

So, let us turn to the elementary school child as a budding materialist and a recipient of The Bribe.

One problem with bribes or rewards is that they fit all too neatly into the competitive nature of things in the classroom. Obviously, too much competition in the classroom is unhealthy and produces undue amounts of pressure on children, hence I do not advocate bribery for good grades or other measures of intellectual ability, because there are many children in every classroom who can never win at this, no matter how hard they try. So I only use bribes in the context of behavior. This way, a child does not have to be smart and clever to win—just good.

GROUP-BUILDING BRIBES

One of the most effective systems I have hit upon is the Table of the Week. During one six-month period, I divided my class into five groups of six children each. The members of each group had their individual desks pushed together so that the six desks formed a "table." I was careful to divide troublemakers, talkers, quiet workers and bright students equally among all five tables, so that each table had a more or less equal chance to win. I also tried to separate children who did not get along well, so that I could keep quarreling at a minimum and avoid comments like "Boy, David, it's all *your* fault that we didn't win this week," and, "Get lost, John, it's *your* fault for bugging *me*" ad nauseum. I also separated cliques and good friends unless the friends worked very well together, in order to keep conversations and chatting down to a reasonable level. I had to spend quite a bit of time observing and analyzing my students before

I put this plan into effect, so that I could come up with an effective seating arrangement. I must give some of the credit for this plan to my students, since it was they who suggested it, in part. Their idea came from a discussion we had in February about how we could keep our room quieter and make better use of our time. In essence, the children's response was, "Pay us to be quieter, and we'll do it." All right, I thought, let's try it and see how it works. It worked for six glorious months, and in Room 8 blissful quiet, calm, and productivity reigned.

We decided to institute a point system for good behavior. Each table had an equal opportunity to win points during the day, and the table that accumulated the highest number of points in five days was designated Table of the Week. The Table of the Week was paid off every Friday with the announcement that its members would receive the coveted privilege of going out to recess first for the next five days. This included free choice of any PE equipment in the ball box. Before each recess during the following week, I would triumphantly announce, "The Table of the Week is excused!", and its members would jauntily saunter past their classmates with exaggerated nonchalance. Then I would dismiss the rest of the class.

I have heard of other teachers using similar ways of assigning rewards. One method that I question is starting with a set number of points, which are reduced whenever a member of a table commits an indiscretion. Taking away points for bad behavior emphasizes the negative, causes hard feelings among the children assigned to a given table and, in the end, leads them to focus their resentment on the teacher: "That old bat! I bet she took away that point just because she hates us." Worst of all, the point-subtraction system makes the teacher a punisher, a penalizer, and a depriver, instead of a giver, a supporter, and a rewarder.

In my system, the number of points awarded varied from time to time but averaged about six points a day. At times, when it appeared that all five tables were outdoing themselves and were doing an equally fine job, I would give every table a point. In most situations, however, one of the five tables really was outstanding, and a single point was awarded to that table.

The points were given for correct behavior in areas that the children and I determined that they needed to work on. We came up with these point-worthy behaviors.

1. Coming in quietly when school starts and being ready to start work. Being on time for school was implicit in this one, and it was amazing how the point system cured some of our habitual laggards for they began to arrive on time, in order not to deprive their table of the coveted early-morning point.
2. A point was given on spelling test days to the table that was able to collect the spelling papers in the most efficient manner. (This was another problem area that the children identified themselves. "Boy, that spelling test collection is sure a bottleneck," remarked one of our class sages and efficiency experts.)
3. A point was given to the table that showed the greatest evidence of working quietly and using time wisely during reading periods. Sometimes I would award an extra point to a table when an individual child had done something outstanding in the way of quiet or conscientious work. I sometimes noticed a particular child who had been reading his book without moving for 25 minutes. His table would be rewarded for his diligence.
4. English was another target area in our room. My class seemed to have a love of creative writing and an abhorrence of grammar (my class the year before had opposite tastes), and a point was awarded to the table who was the most attentive during English. I didn't award this point on the basis of the table who gave the best answers, because here again we would be involving the intelligence factor. Listening and really concentrating was all that was required. Considering the feelings that many of my children had toward English, this was a major accomplishment!
5. Getting ready quietly for recess and coming into the room quietly after recess was another point-worthy situation. In this case, I got more than I bargained for. Children would sit like statues, virtually developing curvature of the spine in their efforts to sit up straight with their hands neatly folded on top

of their desks. Incidentally, I started the folded-hand routine inadvertently, and I finally figured out that I had been communicating in body language. When I wanted my children to listen and be ready for dismissal, I folded my hands in front of my chest. When I finally realized I did this all the time, I knew why my students always folded their hands, too. They were picking up my example. Now that I know I do it, I haven't stopped, because it does look rather nice and official when all the children have their hands neatly folded on their desks. Shades of a convent school!

REWARDS FOR INDIVIDUAL EFFORT

There are other bribes students will work for besides sweets. Another system I have seen used is the individual point system. This technique was employed by one teacher with whom I worked. He used it as a last resort with his low math-group. Each child had his own tally sheet to keep track of the points he earned each day during math. Points were awarded in terms of minutes. When a child had accumulated 15 minute-points, he could cash them in for free time, whenever he chose to do so. This was another "positive point" system, with the points being given for performing correct behavior, rather than being taken away for misbehavior.

Some of the things that were rewarded were:

1. Homework done on time (2 min.).
2. Working quietly for 15 minutes (1 min.).
3. Being a "teacher" and helping someone else in the class who was having difficulties with the work (5 min.).
4. Using the math games in the interest center after one's daily assignment was completed and checked (3 min.).

Serving as a "teacher" did wonders for many of these students' self-images. Even though most of these children were aware that they were in the low math-group, they were able to achieve a great deal of self-respect by being in the position of helping another student in their group. Many of them discovered that they were quite good teachers, a skill that is usually associated with students of greater ability. This tutorial situation seems to work quite well with the less-capable student. It was interesting to note that many of these students used their 15 minute free-time periods to tutor other children, for which they received even more points. The only limits that were placed on the use of the free time were that one could not accumulate more than 15 minutes without cashing them in. This prevented some children from collecting 45 free minutes and thus spending an entire math period in entertainment.

Some other rewards that children might work for are free time at any interest center or activity of their choice, being able to help by correcting papers, getting supplies or running errands or, perhaps, they could earn longer physical education periods if a school's schedule permits. I have heard of classes working together to earn points that would enable them to have a picnic or special outing. The children could then pool their efforts to earn a new game that they would be able to use during their free time.

COLLABORATION IN REWARD SETTING

The best way to determine what bribes you can use with your class is to discover what they consider to be rewarding. One year, my class flatly informed me that it was candy and other edibles that they really craved and were willing to work for. Other groups of children might not have such a sweet tooth, and would want to earn something else. Many groups are not as outspoken in telling you what they consider to be rewarding, so you may have to employ other methods to find out what interests them. One discreet way of making this discovery is to give your pupils an anonymous questionnaire listing various rewards. Ask them to mark the ones that they like best. If they are older students, you could have them rank the list in order of preference.

You don't even have to tell them the purpose of the questionnaire. You could say, "Boys and girls, I'm going to give each of you a list of things that many people your age like to do at school. I want you to circle the things on the list that you would like to do best, if you had the chance," or something to this effect. Then you could tally up the alternatives on a master sheet and determine which rewards are indeed rewarding to the children in your class.

You do not have to reward every single thing that your students do correctly. It is better to reward only those things with which your class seems to be having trouble accomplishing. These areas of concern may change from time to time, and so should your reward system. Maybe your children need to work on working quietly for a couple of months, after which time, they master it to your satisfaction. You might then move on to good sportsmanship in physical education as your target area, and work out a reward system for this. You needn't be the teacher who is dispensing Hershey bars at every turn for every bit of good behavior. This would certainly lose its appeal after a very short period of time, and think of the dental bills you would be heaping on the poor parents!

Children will also work for less-tangible rewards, such as certificates and other official-looking documents to be pinned on their bulletin boards at home or displayed prominently in the kitchen. One school principal had several awards printed up for his teachers to use in rewarding children for various things such as good citizenship, perfect attendance, good sportsmanship, and academic achievement. Children will also respond well to the prospect of your writing a letter home to their parents testifying to their good behavior or to their having completed an outstanding botany project.

THE WHYS AND HOWS OF BEHAVIOR MOD

We have been discussing ways of changing mildly disagreeable behavior in large numbers of children, and now we will change our focus of discussion to ways of changing extremely disagreeable behavior in one individual child. The type of child I have in mind is known as the "chronic misbehaver," "emotionally handicapped," "social misfit," "a holy terror," or "pain in the neck," depending on whether your approach is clinical or informal. We will use professional jargon and call them "emotionally handicapped." Every school has four or five emotionally handicapped children, who are usually on a waiting list for a special education class until the hoped-for opening shows up. This child is biding his time in the regular public school classroom while his teachers and the principal pray for a change in his conduct, the family situation, or a miracle.

The emotionally handicapped child is one who has really severe behavior problems, usually traceable to an unhappy home situation. He is not a child like our friend Manuel in Chapter 1, who misbehaved in a very naughty way nonetheless, but who was basically quite normal in his methods of misbehavior.

The emotionally handicapped child is not normal and tends to do some pretty incomprehensible things. He is usually disliked by his peers and, more often than not, he isn't very pleased with himself, either. He may misbehave in dramatic and serious ways. He may, for example, throw temper trantrums in the classroom, spit at people, or get into bloody fights on the playground. He is often truant. He may be the only child in the third grade who smokes marijuana or writes obscenities on bathroom walls. Your goal is not to play psychiatrist and attempt to unearth all the subconcious motivations that compel him to such things but to help him change his behavior. Knowing a bit about his family situation is desirable, but it really isn't necessary or even helpful to probe his psyche if you want to change his behavior.

Behavior modification in one technique that may work with a youngster like this, but do not feel discouraged if it does not. He may be too much for you to handle, and there is no disgrace in admitting that. But do give behavior modification a try before throwing in the towel.

Before you start a behavior modification program with any child, be certain to discuss his behavior and your plans with your principal. You will also want to involve your school or district psychologist and the child's parents, if possible. Select one behavior that you wish to work on at a time. Do not set out to change a whole list of "deviant" behaviors in one fell swoop. Let's take a look at Mr. Hypothetical Rotten Kid, whom we shall call Joe.

Joe is in the fifth grade and is also on everybody's list of people who should permanently disappear. He teases and annoys other children to distraction, the end result of which usually a fight, in which Joe may even break arms or knock out teeth. He is prone to running madly around the classroom, screaming and breaking objects when things don't go his way. Every time one of his fellow classmates passes by Joe's desk, he pinches and kicks them with gusto. Just looking at Joe makes you want warm his pants or blacken both eyes. However, you are exercising considerable maturity and control, and are determined to give behavior modification a try. You have discussed your plan with the principal, school psychologist, and Joe's mother (his father deserted the family three years ago), and now you are ready to face Joe.

You have selected Joe's angry outbursts and tantrums as the behavior to modify. For the time being, you are going to ignore his kicking, pinching, and fighting, and concentrate only his destructive temper sprees. You begin by observing his temper tantrums over a period of one or two weeks and writing down your observations.

Here are some things to look for when you are observing him. When does he have the tantrums? What seems to precipitate them? Are there any children or adults who seem to set him off more than others? Exactly what does he do during the tantrum? Scream? Lie on the floor? Cry? Smash things? How long do they usually last? Most important, how often do they occur? Daily? Twice a week? Every two weeks? In other words, how much time generally elapses between tantrums?

Now you analyze the data you have been collecting. You discover that Joe tends to blow up about three times a week, usually during research periods in social science when the class is working individually or in small groups on problems of their choice. At this point you may feel like sending Joe to the principal's office during social science, in order to remove him from the tantrum-causing situation, but you won't quit now, will you?

You also notice from your observations that the outbursts begin with Joe's clenching his fists and shutting his eyes tightly. Then he lets out a scream, knocks things off his desk, and throws himself on the floor, screaming and kicking his feet. The incident ends with convulsive sobs and you escorting him out the door, propelling him in the direction of the rest room. When he returns, he is sullen and uncommunicative, staring at the window for the rest of the period.

It would probably be helpful if one or all the people mentioned earlier would attend your conference with Joe. The tone of your discussion is friendly and bussinesslike. You tell Joe that he is behaving in a particular way during social science periods, and that it is important for him to change. You and the other adults present want very much to help him stop this behavior, and you have a plan that you believe will help him. For every 5, 10, or however many minutes you think he can easily handle during social science without this behavior, you will hand Joe a red card. Let's say you have determined that Joe could easily remain calm for 15 minutes without the distinct possibility of a tantrum. The social science period runs one hour. For every three red cards he receives from you, he is permitted to draw dragsters for 10 minutes, or help the custodian, or fingerpaint, or eat a cookie, or do whatever you have previously learned is rewarding to him. This is called a reinforcement schedule, with the drawing or cookie being the reinforcement event. After he has collected 12 cards, he might be able to cash them in for more of the same rewards, or something else, like a bigger candy bar. If he earns 40 cards, perhaps he could cash them in on a toy car or something else that he wants.

You also tell Joe that he must help by letting you know if he feels that he is about to have an outburst. You, of course, are able to tell by his facial expression and fist clenching, but it's important that *Joe* begin to recognize the onset of his tantrums. Maybe he could hold up a blue card or raise both hands, whereupon you will come immediately and say, "Time out." Then you will immediately escort him to the center cubicle or outside the door, where he will remain for five minutes or so, until he is in control of himself once again, and can return to the classroom. You will not reprimand him in any way during the Time Out; you will just remove him from the situation fast! In time, with this technique, it is possible that you can extend the intervals between red cards to a half and hour or maybe even an entire social science period, as Joe becomes more and more able to control his own behavior. The important thing is to start with intervals that Joe can handle, and set goals he can easily reach. No matter how angry you may feel, you must resist the temptation of removing any of Joe's red cards as punishment for any misbehavior that might occur.

Having the principal, psychologists, and parents at the conference helps lend an aura of seriousness and officiality to the proceedings. Your purpose is to insure that everyone, especially Joe, fully understands the rules of the game you and he are about to play. You will probably wish to praise Joe every time you hand him a red card, saying briefly, "You're doing fine, keep it up."

If you succeed in eliminating the tantrums, then you could use the card system to change some of Joe's other deviant behavior. You could award cards for recess periods in which he engaged in constructive play, instead of pinching other children and engaging in fights.

With the kind of behavior modification we have been discussing, it is important to keep in mind that your goal is not so much in eliminating poor behavior but in reinforcing Joe's involvement in satisfactory activity. Actually, the most difficult part of behavior modification is that of *ignoring* negative behavior. If you are concentrating on getting Joe to work on his assignments during social studies (which means "no tantrums" as far as you are concerned), you must ignore him when he falls from grace and lapses into a tantrum. This is hard to do when every fiber in your being wants to grab him and shake him until his teeth rattle. But *any* attention during a tantrum is bound to be reinforcing, and the only thing you can do is to grin and bear it.

It is this ignoring of misbehavior that keeps behavior modification from spreading like wildfire through the schools. Most teachers are willing to reward and reinforce satisfactory behavior once they have caught on to how it is done, but what they find difficult or impossible is looking the other way when a child is engaging in the activity that the teacher is trying to eliminate. The negative behavior is there in the first place because it has a long history of reinforcement, and there is plenty of research with mice and men to show that with negative behavior just an occasional, slight reinforcement is all that is necessary to keep the ball rolling, regardless of whether you are knocking yourself out in rewarding its opposite.

If you attempt behavior modification with an emotionally handicapped child, it may be better to start on one symptom that you may disapprove of but that you can tolerate if there are lapses. In any event, however, you have nothing to lose by rewarding an emotionally handicapped child (or any other child, for that matter) for positive behavior.

If you do institute a reinforcement schedule for Joe, it is important to inform and involve the rest of his classmates in the project. Plan to have him out of the room during the time you are discussing him with the class, in order to avoid a scene or embarrassment. The other children are likely to be agreeable and will not mind the fact that Joe is going to be receiving rewards or privileges that they will not be given. They are just as disturbed about Joe's breaking up the place as you are, and they would like him to change, too. It would certainly make for a more productive social science period without these violent eruptions! They must understand that Joe needs their help, and they are not to tease him or embarrass him in any way about his red cards. They will undoubtedly begin to reinforce him, too, when he begins to accumulate cards. At that time, you might ask Joe if he wishes to cash in some of his cards in the form of a treat for the entire class, like a party or a picnic. This will raise his status immeasurably in the eyes of his peers if Joe's good behavior during social science earns them a cocoa-and-dough-nuts feast or a two-hour softball game!

8

organizing your classroom for learning activities

In the previous chapters I have, perhaps, belabored the point that classroom control is essential if learning is to take place and also that control does not mean yelling at children, punishment, or harsh discipline. It is the teacher who has lost or is losing control when she resorts to such extreme and counterproductive measures.

Control is partly psychological, in the sense that it requires mutual acceptance and respect between teacher and children, but it also requires careful planning and organization. The teacher who has planned and organized has taken much of the unpredictability out of the school day. To be sure, crises and dead-end situations occur even in the best-ordered classrooms, but they are much less frequently encountered when teacher and children know what is supposed to happen next and when the teacher has arranged the daily program and the physical structure of the classroom in such a way that she and the children can interact harmoniously and productively.

First-year teachers are usually so preoccupied with control and discipline problems that they often overlook the more basic need for organization and planning. As a consequence, many teachers do not develop a classroom organization that works for them until their second or third year. Hopefully, my comments in this chapter will alert you to the desirability of starting early with organizing and planning such mundane things like seating arrangements.

What I am about to say assumes that you, like most teachers in the United States and elsewhere, will have what is termed a "self-contained classroom," that is, a conventional teaching situation in which the children are all in the same grade and have you as their teacher for all or most subjects. About 10 percent of American schools have some form of open or un-graded classroom in which children of a fairly wide age span work in groups or independently on learning materials appropri-ate to their educational level. A little over 10 percent or so also have some form of team teaching, in which two teachers col-laborate in planning and supervising learning experiences for (usually) double-sized classroom groups. Such arrangements are innovations that have been introduced within the past decade or so, but their acceptance has not been widespread. If you are to teach in an open or ungraded classroom, much of this chapter will be inappropriate; if you are to team teach, you will, of course, want to work with your partner in determining which of these ideas will be useful.

There are a number of different angles to organizing class-room activities, and I wouldn't want to pretend that the tech-niques I am going to discuss tell the whole story. I always add a number of variations and touches as I proceed through the school year, but the basic structure of my organization depends on the use of monitors, to get children involved and participat-ing; conduct standards to remind children of what is expected of them; and seating arrangements, to channel the flow of class-room activities.

MONITORS, SLAVES, HELOTS, PEONS, AND SERFS

An organizational plan that really works can never be *your* plan. It is bound to fail unless children have a chance to become a living part of it. A monitorial system gives them that oppor-tunity, an opportunity they are eager to take. They seldom have to be persuaded.

Children delight in performing little tasks around the class-room, and alert teachers have, for many decades, taken advan-tage of this built-in eagerness by turning these jobs into monitorships.

It took me quite a bit of fooling around to come up with a

smooth-functioning monitor system. I spent some hours before school began hanging around the instructional materials center in my school district, accosting every teacher who came in, in my attempt to get ideas on monitor systems. I was able to glean enough information to have a system prepared by the first day of school, and the children and I kept changing the system around until we got the bugs worked out of it. So here it is— bug-free. I hope it works for you. At least it is a beginning.

There are 11 monitors in my classroom. The jobs are rotated every two weeks, alternating between boys and girls. If a girl was the Art Supplies Monitor, then she must choose a boy to be her successor. New monitors can only be chosen from the children who have not held the job. This allows every child in the class to have the opportunity of holding the monitorship he desires. I do not use the system of drawing names from a hat to fill the jobs, since you are bound to pull out someone's name for Ball Monitor who has some kind of intense dislike for that position. Whenever I can, I allow the children to make their own decisions.

Here are the monitors I had in my class last year:

1. *Board monitor*. Erases the blackboard, checks chalk supply, gets new pieces from my desk, and keeps the tiny left-over end pieces as a bonus. Cleans erasers.
2. *Door and window monitor*. Opens and closes windows and unlocks and locks door before and after recesses.
3. *Equipment monitor*. Responsible for the care and light maintenance of the many pieces of audio-visual equipment located in our classroom, sets up projector in preparation for films, dusts and covers tape recorder, film strip projector, and record player, and sets up this equipment when needed.
4. *Girls' and boys' line-leaders*.
5. *Ball monitor*. Passes out balls and is responsible for maintaining a sign-out procedure. Must look for missing equipment.
6. *Art supply monitor*. Cleans sink, and distributes and collects all art supplies. Assists in demonstrating art lessons.
7. *Paper monitor*. Passes out paper, including notices to go home. A very busy job!

8. *Messenger and secretary*. Runs errands, answers phone, takes notes during class discussions, is my right-hand man. Highly prestigious job.
9. *Pet monitor*. Cleans guinea pig cage, feeds animals, and handles them.
10. *Lunch monitor*. Takes lunch count and runs it to office. Checks off names before lunch.
11. *Flag salute monitor*. Leads class in the pledge of allegiance every morning. For some reason, it is very low-prestige job.

I really don't think an average classroom needs many more than these monitors. Having monitors certainly saves you from asking 40 times each day, "Who would like to.....?" If you are teaching in the primary grades, you might want to reduce the duties of each monitorship and create more jobs. It is harder for younger children to keep track of too many details.

SETTING STANDARDS FOR CONDUCT

The first thing you need to take care of on the first day of school is to establish the working standards that students are to follow while they are in your class. There are two ways of setting standards: (1) do it yourself and go over your list with your children and (2) have the children set their own standards and make a copy of their list. I use the first method because my standard-setting time is the first 15 minutes of school on Day 1, and I will not run the risk of any fooling around or receiving such cute answers as, "I think it would be neat if everybody talked at once." However, I grant that the second method is more democratic, although you don't fool the children by this sort of ruse. They know what standards you want them to come up with, and they know you will drag it out of them eventually. So I save time and write the list myself.

OUR ROOM STANDARDS

1. We work quietly.

2. We walk in the room and halls.
3. We raise our hands if we want to speak.
4. We listen when someone is speaking.
5. We make good use of our time.
6. We are kind and considerate to everyone.
7. We try to do our best work.

Notice that this list expresses positive actions, instead of such prohibitions as "no talking, no running, no wasting time," and so on. Standards are something that a person strives to live up to, not a list of "don'ts" that nag at you. It is my experience that positive lists of standards get better results in the area of discipline than negative, finger-waggling lists.

Standards should also be invoked in a positive tone. If someone violates a standard, don't pounce on him and crow triumphantly, "Tom, you broke a rule!" All that is necessary is to say, "Tom, I think you need to pay more attention to Standard 2. Try and work on that one today."

Insist that your students live by our standards. In visiting some classrooms, I get the feeling that the teacher and students regard the class standards with a sort of "It would be nice if . . ." attitude. It is no surprise that the children in these classes think that standards are a huge joke. This attitude is to be expected, considering the off-handed attitude that their teachers have about them.

In enforcing standards, please don't resort to the old chestnut of having him write the standards so many hundred times! Instead assign him an essay on, for example, the importance of being kind and considerate to others instead. The latter punishment is likely to have more positive results. At least he will think about the standard. Nobody thinks about anything when writing the same sentence again and again. Such punishments are stupid, in my opinion.

It is effective to write out your standards on a large sheet of lined tag-board and post them in a prominent place in your classroom. Many teachers spend quite a while setting the standards, discussing them, and then promptly forgetting to place them in view. If they are easily visible, you can point them out whenever it is appropriate. I find my standards chart to be one of my most effective means of classroom control.

SEATING ARRANGEMENTS

Fifty years ago, desks fixed to the floor were standard equipment in American schools. The educational innovations of the 1920s changed all that, I am told. It is now possible in most schools to use a variety of seating arrangements, moving chairs and tables around to the position that is most suitable to the activity at hand.

Here are a number of ways of seating arrangements, together with a discussion of advantages and disadvantages of each. The diagrams are for classes of 30 students. The front of the room is at the bottom of each figure.

$$
\begin{array}{ccccc}
X & X & X & X & X \\
X & X & X & X & X \\
X & X & X & X & X \\
X & X & X & X & X \\
X & X & X & X & X \\
X & X & X & X & X \\
\end{array}
$$

Vertical rows (Figure 1). Very traditional. Control facility is excellent. Emphasis is on independent, quiet working. Good for test administration and individualized programs where each child has his own workbook or learning packet. Poor for class discussions or group work of any type.

Horizontal rows (Figure 2). Control facility is very good. Talking occurs between neighbors, not between rows. Good for large group instruction, poor for test administration, art work, or group work of any type.

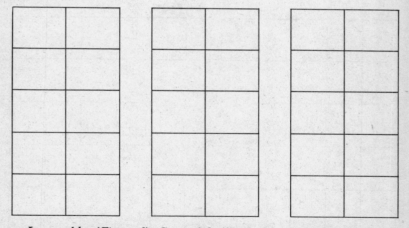

Long tables (Figure 3). Control facility is fair, unless "best table" system is used. (See Chapter 7.) Encourages talking and distractions. Excellent for art projects, and I always use this one at Christmas time. Outstanding for reading activities at three different levels. Poor for committee work because each group is too large.

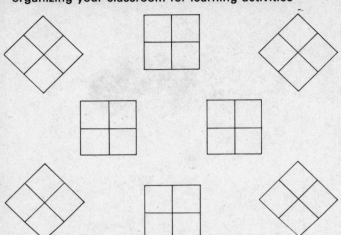

Scattered tables (Figure 4). Control facility can be quite good, if you are careful about who sits where. Outstanding for small group and committee work. Good for art instruction. Poor for class discussions. Adequate for large group instruction, if children all face the same way.

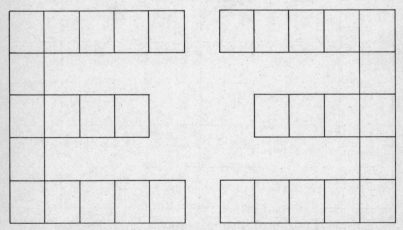

Reverse "E" (Figure 5). Control facility very good. I use this one to begin the school year since it is structured but unconventional. Excellent for instruction and large group discussions. Not bad for art work and for individual projects.

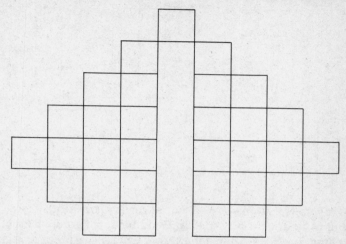

"V" shape (Figure 6). Control facility excellent. Very teacher-directed. Good for large-group instruction and film showings. Poor for art where spillable materials have to be shared.

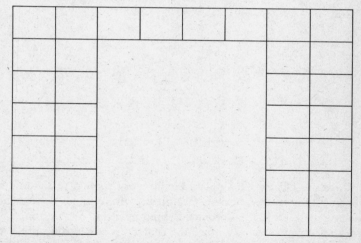

Horseshoe (Figure 7). Control facility adequate, but encourages talking, because of face-to-face arrangement. Excellent for large-group discussions and debates. Good for dramatic role playing activities—use center area for this.

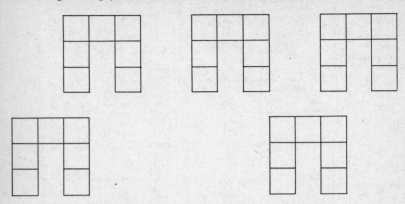

Minihorseshoes (*Figure 8*). Control facility excellent, if you are careful to separate chatty friends. Good for small group instruction and committee work. Good for art work and for sharing of nonspillable materials.

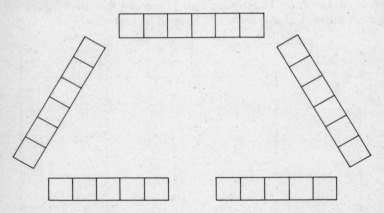

Trapezoid (*Figure 9*). Control facility very good. Outstanding arrangement for dramatics, class meetings, confrontations, debates, and discussions of all kinds—provided children sitting in the front rows turn their chairs around to face the center. In large-group presentations, children in the front rows should face the blackboard. An effective use for primary children is to have them sit on the floor in front of their desks in the flattened oval shape of the interior of the trapezoid.

Semicircle (*Figure 10*). Control facility good, except that note passing is encouraged in upper grades. Like the horseshoe, good for dramatics and discussions. Requires a large room. Poor for individual projects and individualized instruction.

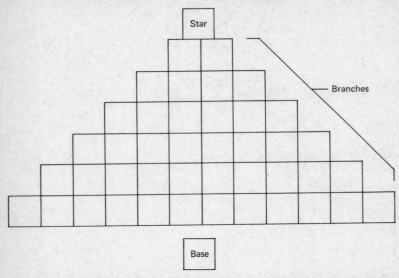

Christmas Tree (Figure 11). A fun arrangement for the holiday season. Included here for variety and change of page.*

WHO TOOK THE GREEN TISSUE PAPER?

You can waste a lot of time chasing around your classroom, looking for misplaced and hard-to-find supplies. Neatness is a trait that is falling into some disfavor lately, with the emphasis being placed on spontaneity, creativity, and unconventionality. However, the best teachers I know are also the tidiest and best organized. Obviously, the rigid and uptight teacher who wastes time endlessly cataloging and stacking supplies isn't going to get off the ground, but neither is the Free Spirit. The disorganized teacher's creative art projects will forever remain a figment of her fruitful imagination because she will be spending the entire art period searching the classroom and the school for the necessary supplies. Well-organized teachers have the freedom

---

*Thanks to Sharon Kelley, Gates School, San Joaquin Elementary School District, El Toro, Cal.

to be spontaneous and creative, because they are able to lay their hands on any supplies at a moment's notice. These are the only teachers who can act on the spur-of-the-moment idea that it would be fun to make little ghosts to illustrate Halloween poems, because they know where the white tissue paper is and they know there is enough paper for every child's experiment in ghost making.

Allow me to list some supplies which I feel every elementary school teacher needs to keep on hand in his classroom. These supplies should be stored neatly, accessibly, and if they are on shelves or in boxes, those containers should be clearly labelled, in order that students, substitutes, and you can find them quickly. If you cannot get these items from your principal or school supply room, don't rush out and purchase them. I am merely suggesting.

- Colored construction paper, 20 sheets of each color.
- Felt pens for lettering, preferably the nonpermanent kind.
- Manila drawing paper, about 40 sheets.
- Newsprint, for tempera painting.
- Watercolor paper.
- Modelling clay.
- NEWSPAPERS !!! They have 1000 uses.
- School paper for writing assignments, unless your school requires that the children supply their own.
- Pencils.
- Crayons.
- Tagboard for making charts.
- Scissors, preferably one pair for each child.
- Tempera paint.
- Brushes.
- Paste.
- Nontoxic glue (children prefer this to paste).
- Masking tape.
- Clear cellophane tape.

All these should be readily located by children so that they are not running up to interrupt your reading lesson with plaintive cries, "Where's the jar of paste?."

If you have students coming to you from other classrooms, labeling the whereabouts of important supplies is doubly important. If I only had a penny for every time a child who came to my room for science and said, "I forget where you keep your paper. . . ." So I gave up my fictitious pennies, and clearly labeled the paper cupboard. It is the responsibility of the paper monitor to keep this cupboard neatly organized and to inform me when we are short of anything. Occasionally, the monitor or I would forget, and a-borrowing we would go, but at least we had made the effort. There is almost nothing a teacher dislikes more than interruptions like, "Mrs. Fisk wants to know, do you gots (sic!) any yellow paint?" Teachers who continually send their students parading through the school borrowing supplies in the middle of class rapidly become very unpopular, and other teachers begin to hold out on them. Even if they have plenty of glue they will tend not to send it over to Mr. Davis. "Let him get his own glue for a change," they think. "Why should I carry him along?" On the other hand, if you are miserly and self-righteous and never lend supplies to anybody, you will have no one to bail you out when you get caught short, which is bound to happen to the best of us once in a while.

Here is a second group of supplies that are well worth keeping in your classroom. Keep a box of drawer labelled "Scraps," in which you instruct your students to place the leftover bits of construction paper from their artistic efforts. You will be teaching them frugality and will be doing your fellow taxpayers a service, too. Pieces of fabric and notions like lace, rickrack, and ribbon are good to save and keep handy as well. And here are some other items: cereal cartons and shoe boxes to be used for dioramas or shadow boxes; large three-pound coffee cans for mixing paint or storing leftover crayons; and plastic margarine containers with lids for storing paste and paint.

A good way to keep scissors, if each child does not have his own, is to use a shoe box with a lid. Tape the lid on securely with masking tape. Cover the whole box with heavy construction paper, and make as many little slits through the lid as you have pairs of scissors. Stick the scissors in the box point down, so their handles are protruding from the slit.

One method of organizing your teaching supplies is to use a large carton for each subject area. You could have one carton labeled "Reading," another, "Math," another, "Art," and so on. Inside the carton, you can place manila file folders in which you can store dittos and notes without wrinkling. You can also keep games, bulletin board materials, and other related items in the same carton.

After you have started to accumulate more material on each subject, you might wish to devote one carton to each unit in a particular area of the curriculum. You could have one entire carton labeled "Plants," another labeled "Animals," another labeled "Solar System," and so on, for the rest of your science and social studies units. When you are going to teach the unit again, all you have to do is pull out the carton, and there is most of the planning already done for you.

9

the first day of school
and what to do about it

It is late August, and you are dreaming of the First Day of School—and, if you are like many who are teaching for the first time, your dreams run to nightmares of unruly classes, losing your nerve and quitting, coping with a gruff, short-tempered principal, and so on. But hang on, all is not lost, and in a few days or weeks, you will be able to look back on your intial encounter with some pride and, perhaps, even with an amused detachment.

I can look at my own First Day of School with some pride and amused detachment now but, at the time, I found it devastating. (In fact, one of the reasons I have written this book is to provide young teachers with the kind of advice I wish I had received.) My initial error consisted of overanticipating the ability of my pupils, who became upset when they were able to do well on the activities I had planned. I now realize that the questionnaire I gave them to complete was far too long for nine-year-olds. Then, the little incident of having Manuel defy me, which I described in Chapter 3, shook me up a great deal. Nor was my confidence in facing the class helped by the fact that when I was waiting in the classroom for school to begin, some of my students-to-be amused themselves by running back and forth outside the window, making noises of disgust and disdain. Since then, I have realized that these children were just letting off steam and that they were, in actuality, quite nervous and worried about an imminent encounter with their new teacher. If I had known this, I would not have taken their foolishness personally, my feelings would not have been hurt, and I could have faced the class with more self-assurance.

Actually, I think I did a good job and made a decent impression on the children that first day but, at the time, I did not think so. I was saved by the fact that I had done a considerable amount of preplanning of activities, but I had no reason to believe that I had done the right thing, having nothing to go on and not knowing how to evaluate the children's reactions. At the end of the day, I sat in the back row at the faculty meeting, depressed and wanting to cry. Then I went home and collapsed. I thought of quitting right then and there, but my husband's supportive arguments and my own common sense convinced me that I was overreacting. In my heart I knew that the First Day of School was over, that it would be easier from now on, and that nothing I had done the first day was so bad that it could not be retrieved. I was still feeling my way by the end of the first week, but by then my normal self-confidence had returned, the children and I had gotten to know each other, and the classroom activities were beginning to move into productive channels. But let us consider ways first-day anxieties can be avoided, or at least reduced.

PRELIMINARY ANXIETIES AND FRUSTRATIONS

Let us say that you, a new teacher, have visited the school where you are to teach, have met the principal, the office staff, some of the teachers, and have seen your classroom in its stark summer nakedness. In your mind's eye, you see yourself teaching 30 enthralled youngsters, but what you cannot see is how it all starts. At least, I couldn't see myself conducting the opening day of school. I hadn't the remotest idea of what I would be doing, and I had only 10 days to come up with something.

As much as I came to like my fellow teachers later, I found them to be of little help during this period. For one thing, I had only just met them and did not know where their strengths lay. Furthermore, they were preoccupied and busy with their own preparations. When I asked one teacher what I should do the first day, she replied blithely, "Survive it!" and breezed away, giggling, leaving me more anxious and depressed than ever.

Others told me that my first day should be spent distributing materials and supplies (which?), passing out textbooks (what ones and to whom?), setting standards (how?) and establishing a "climate of firm, friendly control and productivity" (help!).

The first day, I was assured, was critical in setting the tone of the ensuing school year because a poor first impression is hard to overcome. Smile a lot, a teacher told me. Make the boys and girls feel secure and welcome. Give them things to look forward to, to anticipate. Make them feel that this year is going to be fun and exciting.

Ridiculous, said others. Be firm and rigid the first day. Don't appear to be a pushover or you will get trouble for sure. If you are nice and sweet and all smiles, the children won't respect you and will take you for a simpering fool. Don't emphasize fun and excitement—school is work, work, and more work, and it is wrong to mislead your students into thinking that this year is going to be a barrel of laughs and entertainment.

Each of these bits of advice has a kernel of truth in it, and each has obvious deficiencies if followed exclusively. Everyone has to develop a teaching style of his own, of course, but most teachers I know who have had successful First Days adopted an approach that was both friendly and authoritative and that was also warm and firm.

You will have only one First Day of School. After that, it will be much easier. The first day and the next and following years will be nothing compared to the first, because you will have a better idea of what you are doing and will know what to expect. So be of good cheer, pull yourself together, and start to make your lists.

Your first list consists of the things you need to do before the first day of school in order to be ready to receive your pupils. The second list is the things you are going to do on the First Day. The third list covers the entire first week.

CHECK LIST FOR THE FIRST DAY

This list will obviously vary from school to school and area t0 area, but I am certain most of the items will be the same wherever you are.

1. Check the contents of the classroom cupboards and yourself find out whether the supplies are appropriate for your grade level. If not, find out how to dispose of them and where the right books and materials can be obtained.
2. Obtain the correct textbooks for your grade level in sufficient quantity for the number of pupils you will have. If you can, get a few extra books in case there are students who were not preenrolled. If the school is short of the prescribed books, find out what can be used as a temporary substitute. Who to ask? Other teachers at your grade level, the school librarian, and the office staff.
3. Lay in a supply of construction paper, writing and drawing paper, scissors, crayons, paint, paste, glue, and pencils. Place one sharpened pencil and one box of crayons in each desk. This saves distributing these items on the first day and is also a nice touch, showing the students that you were expecting them.
4. Check your own desk for a stapler, good scissors, pins, chalk, and felt-tipped marking pens. If they are not there, get them from you school secretary or from the person who issues supplies.
5. Measure the bulletin board spaces and write down the dimensions to assist yourself in planning what to put up.
6. Ask what supplementary materials or devices (films, tape recorders, special interest book, and so on) are available.

If your school district has issued you a curriculum guide, it will help you with much of the above.

SETTING THE STAGE

By now you have completed the preplanning stage and are ready to place the props on the stage in their proper places for Act One.

7. Stack neatly on a counter or table, all the textbooks you are

planning to distribute on the first day of school. In schools I have taught in, the list would include a spelling book, a handwriting book and, perhaps, a health or science book. In the fifth or sixth grade, a history or a social studies book would also be included. Be sure you have a reason for distributing these books—don't give them to the children unless they are going to be used. If you are not planning to use the math books until Wednesday, for example, wait until Wednesday before you give them out.

8. Arrange the desks in one of the seating arrangements found in Chapter 8. (I like the Reversed E, for the reasons I mentioned.) Plan a seating chart and make name tags for the desks. Lay the name tags on the desks but don't attach them until the first day. (This is because you might place a big child at a little desk.) You might read through the cumulative records before doing the seating arrangement in order to anticipate any problems that might occur if Victor sits next to Swen, for instance. (See Chapter 13 on cumulative records.) Children with vision or hearing problems should be placed toward the front of the classroom. I try to seat shyer and less mature children toward the front also because being closer to the teacher usually makes them feel more secure.

9. Move into your room, bringing whatever personal teaching supplies you want to store in your classroom.

10. Make up and post your standards chart and list of monitors.

11. Set up one general free-time learning center for those students who finish things early. They won't have library books to read this first week, so something must be provided for them to do when they complete work before the other children. Some things they could do would be jigsaw puzzles, coloring pages, simple craft projects, books to look at, and educational games and "brain-teaser" puzzles.

12. Make your bulletin boards and put them up. Beginning-of-the-year bulletin boards should be colorful, gay, and eye-catching. There are many clever ideas in books about bulletin boards.

WRITING THE SCRIPT

You are now ready to plan the first day and week of school. After you have deliberated and worked over this list, you will be ready to fill in your lesson plan book for the first week. These are the things that you should be doing on the first day of school.

1. Introduce yourself to your students.
2. Take the roll and ask who has recently moved to the area and who is new.
3. Go over the room standards (see Chapter 8) and your own rules (like "no gum").
4. Go over the general regulations of the school and the school's rules regarding playground behavior. Your principal will most likely tell you what he wishes you to say to your pupils on this score.
5. If you are teaching in grades three to six, a brief personal questionnaire is a good activity for the first day. It is easier for most children to fill in answers about their favorite hobbies and pets and their families than to have their teacher say, "Write a story telling me all about you."
6. Don't assign an essay on "What I did last summer." By the second grade, most children are thoroughly sick of that old chestnut, and it is very embarassing for children who did not do any traveling during the summer. Nobody likes to write, "I didn't do nothing, I just stayed home," when the child sitting next to him is going into fascinating details about his trip back to Arkansas to visit his cousins or a trip into Mexico or French Canada.
7. Pass out the textbooks you are actually going to use on the first day, one set at a time.
8. You might begin your diagnostic testing by administering a group test. I wouldn't give any individual tests on the first day of school. It is sort of frightening for some children to have encounter their new teacher on a one-to-one basis on the very first day of school.
9. Try to have a couple of brief "fun" activities like simple art projects or a little game for younger children. Finger plays are

good for kindergarten, first, and second grades. When you are playing a game with your students on the first day, take that opportunity to establish very clear rules as to how you want the children to behave. Do not tolerate any roughhousing, shouting, or talking out of turn because then you will only be setting the stage for worse misbehavior later in the week. If your students get carried away with themselves during such activities on the first day, warn them once, and if the undesirable behavior continues, stop the activity and go on immediately to something else. You have now established yourself as a Person who Means What She Says.

10. Have a few short Real Work type lessons for the first day. Get the point across to the children that they are here to learn, and that the learning is going to begin immediately. Make the lessons simple but not too easy. You don't want to give the impression that school this year is going to be a breeze, nor do you want to scare any of the less-able students.

11. Read a brief story or start a book. For the primary grades, I would select a book with lots of pictures, and maybe one with an amusing but not too uproarious plot.

12. Some principals I know think that it is important to send one paper home with your students on the first day. This shows the parents that nobody was wasting time by playing all day. It also makes it clear to the parents that you are eager to set up good school-home communications with them. It shows the child that you expect him to bring home work on a regular basis. Bringing a paper home is a good prop for the child to use when he is asked, "What did you do on the first day of school?"

13. It is better to overplan for the first day than to be caught short without adequate lessons and activities. If you are at a loss as to what to do, students come to feel as though their teacher doesn't know what to do next. You want them to feel that you *do* know what to do next for the rest of the year. But do it leisurely, whatever you can accomplish.

CHECKLIST FOR THE REST OF THE WEEK

Your list for the rest of the first week of school will contain items such as diagnostic testing in reading, math, English, and spelling. If you are teaching first grade, you had better plan a few large-group phonics lessons until you have determined the level of readiness of each child. You should begin a couple of easy units in social studies and science. Safety at school and home is always a good starting point in science and health, and map study is a good opener for social science.

If you are going to get involved in team teaching, it is better not to launch into a long unit of study. Select something that can be wrapped up quickly if necessary when the teaming is ready to begin.

By the beginning of the second week of school you should have a pretty good idea of how well each of your children reads. If they are to be ability-grouped for reading and will be going to different teachers, form your list of who will be placed in which group. If your classroom is self-contained in reading, you can start forming your groups or begin your individualized program.

The remainder of the first week can be devoted to setting room standards in greater detail than you were able to do on the first day of school. You can begin to teach your children how to prepare their written work, where to put it when finished, when they can leave their seats, how they behave at the learning center, what they do when their work is finished, and what sort of work habits you want them to adopt. On the first Friday, I would suggest sending home a dittoed newsletter to parents describing some of the things you and their children did during the first week of school.

PREPARING BODY AND SOUL

I find the first day of school goes a lot better if one has eaten lightly and has had plenty of rest the week before, and especially the night before. If you are a woman, I think you should certainly buy something new to wear on the first day of school. Little girls seem to respond well to pink, lavender, or purple, and they will shyly tell you that they like your dress, if you choose something in one of these colors. I would not wear anything dark or somber in color on the first day of school, nor would I wear anything too busy or wild in color, like a dress that is a riot of reds, oranges, and yellows. Clothing is always very important in teaching, and a great deal of thought should go into looking as sharp and well-coordinated as possible. No matter how hot it is, I think the men should wear a tie on the first day of school. After all, your boys and girls have been stuffed into their brand-new back-to-school outfits by their parents, so you should look equally well-turned out. A beginning male teacher's concession to physical preparation for the first day of school should be the purchase of a new tie and shirt at least.

Now that you are nicely rested and have purchased and planned your outfit, you must now make your mental preparations. Keep in mind that you do not have to set the world on fire on the first day of school. You just have to get through it in reasonably good shape. Actually, your students are just as apprehensive and concerned about the first day of school as you are. Many children are afraid of new teachers and are worried about liking their teacher and having their teachers like them. Families reinforce this concern, and often children are asked when they return home from the first day of school, "Do you like your teacher?" You would like them to answer, "Yes, but she's strict" and never, "No, I hate her. She's so mean." Nor do you want them to say, "Yes, she's really far out. You can do anything you want, and it doesn't shake her up!"

The impression you are trying to give on the first day of school is that you are both a friendly and a firm teacher, and that school is going to be both enjoyable and serious. You want your students to realize that they are there to learn above all. Having fun is definitely a by-product of busy, satisfying experiences. Hence "fun and games" receive little stress on the first day of school to avoid giving children a false impression of the way things are going to be in your class.

Here is an idea of something you can say in the way of

opening remarks on the first day of school. You can adapt it to fit the needs of your grade level. "Good morning, boys and girls. My name is Mr/Miss/Mrs/Ms Goodheart, and I'm going to be your teacher this year. I'm very happy to see each and every one of you here today, and I'm very glad to be here because I know I am going to like being your teacher."

Some teachers like to add a few comments to let their students know that how amiable or strict they are going to be depends on how well the class behaves. I think such remarks are worth making, since they really are true. A teacher's attitude and behavior is shaped largely by the attitudes and behavior of his students. It is quite appropriate to remind them of this fact. In doing so, you also let the children know that you are very aware of their apprehensions and worries about you and the ensuing school year.

"I know many of you are wondering if I will be very nice or if I will be not so nice. Well, I'll tell you a secret—it all depends on you! If all of you behave yourselves and try your best, then I know you will enjoy being in our class."

Once introductory remarks are out of the way, you can forge ahead with taking the roll, saying the Pledge of Allegiance, and other business details. You will be surprised at how smoothly the first day of school will go, once you have passed the initial few moments of mutual sizing up between teacher and children.

10

structured and unstructured approaches

IN DEFENSE OF BOOKS

When I was a child in elementary school, most of our social studies consisted of taking turns at reading the textbook aloud, page by page, to the rest of the class. For an exciting break in this deadly routine, we got to answer the questions at the back of the chapter. It was probably this type of textbook use that led some educators to denounce textbooks as detrimental to significant learning. As a result of this antitextbook movement, we now have a few young teachers who reject textbooks altogether and are committed to the exclusive use of such interpersonal techniques as encounter groups, group discussion, role playing, and psychological games. My feeling is that there is a time and a place for such approaches, and that they can be used more extensively in some schools than in others, but that books are absolutely essential if children are to learn what they need to know and what we have every reason to expect them to learn.

This does not mean that textbooks should be used exclusively. There are many ways that subjects can be taught and learned—motion films, filmstrips, audiotapes, research projects, dramatics, arts and crafts, group discussions, field trips, and physical demonstrations are all possible. There is no reason, however, why textbooks should be excluded from this list. Most of them, after all, are very well thought out and give continuity and structure to the information, ideas, and insights that both teacher and pupil can pick up from other sources and experiences. If they are not overused or overstressed, textbooks can provide a firm background or a starting point for significant learning.

Textbooks, like any other teaching-learning device, are not

problem-free. For one thing, you will probably find that a sizable percentage of your students are unable to read them. You give your third-graders some questions on insects, whereupon some two thirds of them, for example, eagerly turn to their science books and start looking up answers. The other third stare at you blankly or start looking for interesting activities that have nothing to do with learning about insects.

"Find an alternative," say the experts. "Let them look in other sources for the necessary information."

But where can these poor readers turn? To the encyclopedia? Not likely, inasmuch as it is probably written at the eighth-grade level. To other science books? Same problem there as with the texts, since they are written at the third-grade level or higher.

It is problems like these that try teacher's souls. My solution has been to rewrite sections of the state-prescribed textbooks and other books, using words appropriate to the reading levels of my less-expert readers. Although this takes time, it is not very difficult—even a third-grade teacher can write at the second grade level! I have found rewrites a useful technique, even for average and above-average readers, when I want to make information available that has appeared in a periodical or book for adults. For example, I managed to water down some fairly complicated information on the polution problem in rivers and lakes, information that simply was not available in the textbook and other references available to my fourth-graders.

I think it is a good idea to rely on textbooks at the beginning of your first year, at least until you get your feet wet. Then you can begin to explore other ways of presenting information and concepts. Don't let people make you feel guilty and inadequate for using textbooks.

UNITS: PLANS AND PROCEDURES

Instructional units are the most widely used approaches to teaching the subject matter areas. The idea is to collect piles of information on a particular subject, get deeply involved in it for two weeks at least, and then move on to another subject, using the same technique. You can usually tell what units a teacher is doing when you walk into his classroom. If serapes are hanging over the blackboard, colorful gourds and sombreros are fetchingly displayed all over the room, and common classroom objects bear little Spanish name tags it would be superfluous to ask what these children are studying in social studies. Upon entering some classrooms, you feel like you have wandered into the Teahouse of the August Moon or Trader Vic's Polynesian Restaurant. Such trappings add reality and interest to the subject matter at hand. Some school systems supply their teachers with outlines of the units that are to be covered in the grades they are teaching and even do some supervising to ensure that the units are taught or covered. A great many systems, however, assume that teachers will take the initative to organize and set up units that are appropriate to the state- or system-prescribed textbooks they are using. There are advantages and disadvantages to both approaches. Unit prescription and supervision can be useful, especially for new teachers, but my own preference is for the freedom and latitude that teachers enjoy in the schools in which I have taught. The lack of structure gives teachers more of a chance to innovate, in my opinion.

Let us assume that the decision as to what units you will teach is yours. One of your first duties (of first duties there is no end!) should be that of mapping out the units that you plan to teach during the year. Using the textbook as a guide, write down the units you hope to cover, and how many weeks you will be devoting to each one. Some are worth more than other. For example, I have found in my science curriculum that the Space Unit I teach is worth a good eight weeks, but Light and Sound can be easily covered in four. Then you shuffle the order of the units around until you know generally what you will be teaching when. This enables you to order films to go with your units, with some chance that they might arrive on time to be relevant. Bear in mind that a unit almost always takes longer than you have planned. When you have decided which units will come first chronologically, you can begin detailed planning of the first two units that you are going to teach.

You must first set your goals—that is, what information and-

/or skills do you want your students gain from studying this subject? What main points or concepts do you wish to cover? Are you interested in giving them a quick overview, or will the unit go into more detail? Second, you can take a look at the state textbook and note the pages that deal with your proposal subject matter. Then read the appropriate related pages in the teacher's edition of the textbook. Teacher's editions are valuable source of information and ideas that many teachers overlook in their drive to be creative. I have found some marvelous ideas for projects, experiments, and learning center activities in teacher's editions. Decide how you will introduce the unit. One tried-and-true way is to put up a motivating bulletin board one week before you take up the subject as a kind of "tease" that will entice your youngsters to want to learn more about the topic. You could also set up some sort of learning center activity—nothing elaborate, just something simple and seductive. Let's say you are starting a unit on Nigeria. Your first learning-center activity might be the construction of an African mask made out of paper plates and string.

The next step would be to order your films. Try to have no more than two films coming each week. Because of problems inherent in the procurement of films, this, of course, is an ideal that you will never attain, but it is a nice idea anyway. Incidentally, call them "films," not "movies," and be sure they are used educationally and not as entertainment.

And look into the availability of *realia*. Realia consist of teaching displays that are not tapes, records, printed matter, or photography. They are "real," like a Japanese kimono, a bag of sand from the Gobi Desert, or a Kachina doll. Tangible objects help a great deal in making your point clear to children, and they will also help them to remember things they have read or heard.

A master list of all the activities and projects that will be part of this unit is the next organizational step. Write down all the related art projects that you want to do during the unit, all the learning activities (write a report on volcanoes, outline Chapter 3, draw a diagram of the heart, and act out skits of Samoan family life, for example) that will be included in the unit. Now all you need to do is to shuffle them into a good sequence, fill in your plan book, and go to it, Teach! Repeat the same procedure about three weeks before you begin each new unit, and the staff will marvel at your competence. "You'd never know you were just a first-year teacher," they will say.

BRAINWASHING, SELF-TAUGHT

Sooner or later, team teaching notwithstanding, you will be forced to teach a subject that either turns you off or that you know absolutely nothing about. Since the elementary school teacher is expected to be a jack-of-all-trades and master of them all, and since the people down in Central Office believe that there is nothing in the elementary school curriculum that a little general knowledge won't cover, it stands to reason that you are fated to encounter a gap in your educational background. My own informal surveys show that most elementary schoolteachers enjoy teaching reading, art, and physical education. Social studies runs a good second followed by math, science, music, handwriting, spelling and creative writing. Grammar is the least favored subject. By some odd coincidence, elementary school children also list reading, art, physical education, and social studies as their favorite subjects, although I must admit that I am encouraged by my discovery that there are more and more children who like math and science. Let us say that you are one of those who feel inadequate with any and all mathematical formulations and consequently hate the thought of teaching math. As a matter of fact, you got a C+ (or was it a B—?) in college algebra by dint of hard work, getting all your homework in on time, trying to ask the instructor intelligent questions, and getting one or two more able students to explain things to you after class. When the course was over, you breathed a sigh of relief at your passing grade and promptly forgot everything you had learned.

If this is in any respect true of you, welcome to the group! Math is a subject that has always eluded my comprehension. This is a strange state of affairs, because I enjoy and do well in science (as long as no calculations are involved), but math and

I have been enemies for a long time. Hence, I knew I had to sell myself on math before I could motivate my math students to work at it and learn the math in the fourth-grade textbook.

I first underwent a period of self-induced brainwashing and conditioning, a necessary step in talking oneself into liking any hated subject in the curriculum. I forced myself to look at the textbook and went through it chapter by chapter. What I discovered was that concepts intended for fourth-graders really could be understood by an average adult like myself, even one with a math block. It then occurred to me that most of my difficulties were encountered after elementary school, when such things as working with formulas and quadratic equations were the order of the day. Then I practiced explaining the first two chapters of the text to myself, until I was certain that I understood both the material and my explanations.

Now I was ready for Phase 2. I sought to discover just what it was about math that turned math lovers on. If you are trying to learn to like something that you have long hated, you must first accept the fact that there are a lot of people in the world who like it. After you have swallowed that unbelievable fact, you are able to delve deeply into the reasons why these people like that subject. The best way is to ask probing questions of these individuals. Most people can come up with some reasons why they enjoy something. In psyching out math lovers, I found out that they thought math was exciting, challenging, and interesting, because it was concrete and clear. There is a certain security in knowing that every problem has a correct answer, which is always there for the person who seeks it. Math people are problem-solvers, and they like to sneak off in corners by themselves and try alternate approaches, until they came up with the right solution. They also like to do puzzles and play logic games, like chess. Math people like to work alone and do not enjoy group problem-solving efforts. They also like the challenge of figuring things out for themselves and do not like overprotective teachers and friends who want to help them out. Now I could see the math lovers' point of view, and there is certainly something in it. Of course it goes without saying that if you are not good at empathizing, this approach will not work for you. But them, if you are not empathic, what are you doing in teaching?

The point in empathizing with math people is that not only did I discover what is likable about the subject, but I also learned how math people think. To do a really good job of teaching math, it helps to think like a math person. This project also gave me ammunition, terminology, and ideas when it came to actually teaching math.

Phase 3 was a little warm-up exercise I did before each math lesson. I went through these mental calisthenics quite religiously.

"Oh boy," I simpered, "Time for good old math. I can hardly wait for recess to be over so I can start multiplying. Isn't this exciting?"

Sometimes I said these ridiculous things aloud to my class. At first I was surprised to find that they did not consider them as foolish and empty as they seemed to me. In fact, their response was so favorable that I went even further. When it came to explaining the intricacies of determing the area of rectangles, I became dramatic, eloquent, and—I am afraid to say—hammy. (Actually, I think there is a little of the ham actor in every successful teacher.)

To my amazement, it worked. I convinced not only the children but myself as well that math is not a thing to be feared, and that it is actually interesting and even fascinating. Later, I learned that what I had done was actually a form of psychological role-playing, one of the most powerful of all attitude changers, and one that has been used successfully in group therapy, in behavior modification, and in getting people to stop smoking or overeating.

THE TOTAL IMMERSION WAY TO EXPERTISE

It is infinitely easier to learn to teach subjects you know nothing about if you can approach them without panic or animosity. My favorite technique is total immersion, an idea I borrowed from the Berlitz language schools. The first step it to get thee to a library and start reading and looking through the *Reader's Guide to Periodical Literature* for anything related to the topic. If there are films, audiovisual aids, displays, or exhibits, so much the better.

Although I had been a history major in college, Pre-Colombian Mexico somehow had been overlooked, and my first unit assignment in student teaching was, you guessed it, the Aztecs. Aztec was a word I remembered vaguely from the distant past (probably sixth grade), but that was about all. I was tempted to ask to teach something else, on the grounds that I know nothing about the Aztecs but, instead, I went to the University library, and began my pre-Colombian total immersion. Although my stomach was turned by accounts of Aztec religious customs, I found other aspects of their culture quite interesting. At the same time I realized that my sixth-grade boys would be just as attracted by descriptions of gory sacrifices and slayings as I was repelled by them, and I knew a selling point when I saw one.

The Aztecs were a warlike people, and it occurred to me that boys would also be interested in their battle tactics and military organization. I knew that accounts of the daily life and family customs would interest the girls in my class. The stories of the gods and legends sounded as though they would intrigue both boys and girls and, needless to say, the unit was a great success. What started out as a big blank in my liberal education became an exciting adventure in learning for the children and myself as well.

I recommend total immersion tactics to anyone who wants to develop interesting, exciting units and also to broaden his mind. Just think of what a fascinating conversationalist you will become after you have been teaching a few years! One year, I developed some expertise in physical and historical geology, Japanese and Nigerian culture, Latin American music, and the rudiments of electricity just because I had to teach units on these subjects.

11

what do I do now?

Into every teacher's life, a little rain must fall and, in some parts of the country, a little snow and sleet will fall, too. And on you falls the burden of controlling and/or entertaining your boys and girls at recess on those days. Or maybe your lesson went much faster than you thought it would and you are left with 15 minutes to kill and 30 restless students waiting for recess. Perhaps a school assembly cut into your reading period, and now you have to back-paddle until lunch time. I notice that at times like these, many beginning teachers lose some of their hard-earned control. These situations cry out for entertainment! If you can educate and enlighten at the same time that's all to the good, but be willing to settle for sheer fun and games, because you are lucky to salvage your control under such adverse and potentially overstimulating circumstances.

Rainy-day recesses can be spent playing such games as Who's Got the Button? (or the keys or the eraser), Seven-Up, Twenty Questions, or People Tic-Tac-Toe (for this one, you arrange three rows of three chairs each in an open space in the classroom, and divide the class sexes to compete against each other. When your children get good at this, you will have lots of Cat's Games). You can pull educational games from your learning centers and ask the children to raise their hands if they want to play a particular game. Be sure you structure things very carefully if you're going to have more than one activity going on at the same time. Charades and other pantomime games are great to fill in a few minutes here and there. Acting out difficult situations is great catharsis for the children, also. You can ask for a volunteer to pantomime a mother's reaction to a bad report card or a teacher breaking up a fight on the playground. You can always justify this educationally on the grounds of developing empathy and social awareness.

Older students can use spare moments to practice discussion skills. It takes a dynamic leader to control open discussions among students, so don't attempt this unless you really know what you are doing. A new teacher I knew used to end the school day with a 15 minute rap session on anything the kids wanted to talk about, but this quickly got out of hand simply because she didn't know how to lead and channel discussions. Furthermore, she had not spent enough time going over ground rules for open discussions with the children. There were also (and will always be) several students who took advantage of the situation to make remarks that were insulting to other students and unnecessarily vicious. Because the teacher had invited the children to "get things off your chest," and "say anything you want," this put her in the situation of condoning and supporting what was said. There is a place for no-holds-barred hostility— in group therapy sessions conducted by a skilled practicioner —but a 15 minute ad hoc classroom discussion is not the place. In well-run classrooms, learning experiences will have a thera- peutic (i.e., positive healing) effect on many a child, but this is true of many types of adult-child encounters. A teacher is not a psychotherapist and shouldn't try to be one. This role calls for expertise, proper resources, and unlimited time.

Be cautious, also, about encouraging too open a discussion of such topics as "What I Dislike about my Parents," because you may find out many things you didn't want to know, with repercussions in the form of phone calls from irate parents.

TELL ME A STORY

Story-time is a well-established feature in the daily life of early primary grades, but many educators overlook the need for this kind of activity in the upper elementary grades. Reading aloud to your class accomplishes many positive things, and I would like to make a pitch for a regular story period throughout the elementary school program.

For one thing, a regular story period introduces security and continuity into your program. It gives your students a regular and predictable event to look foward to. Almost every child I know between the ages of 3 and 13 loves to have someone read to them. Children find it soothing, relaxing, and enthralling.

But these are not the most important reasons why you should read daily to your class. All teachers and most students intrinsically believe that reading is a means to an end. For a few children, learning to read is an end in itself—one learns to read because one is expected to learn, period. The majority of youngsters realize that learning to read is necessary in that it opens up vast stores of information. You read to find out things. It soon becomes pretty obvious to every school-age child that 75 percent of what one does in school depends upon reading. Hence, the reason you read to your class is to encourage the love of books. By selecting interesting books you can subtly convey to your children that reading gives one great pleasure. Many teachers talk a good line to their students on the subject of "reading is fun," but they seldom demonstrate their own love of literature. A teacher reading aloud, displaying obvious enjoyment in the book, and the very act of reading is an unbeatable model for behavior.

The best books to read to your children are not necessarily the so-called children's classics, many of which I have found to be too long to hold the interest of all but sixth-grade students. Some educators recommend selecting books whose vocabulary level is at least one year above that of your students. This is good idea for expanding the horizons of the more capable child, but you will lose the attention of your more limited students if you aim too far over their heads. It is not easy to find books that appeal to both sexes, especially beyond the early primary grades. Some novels my students have enjoyed are *Charlotte's Web, Pinnochio, Black Beauty, Chitty Chitty Bang Bang, James and the Giant Peach, Charlie and the Chocolate Factory* (the latter two by Roald Dahl), and *The Mouse and the Motor-cycle* by Beverly Cleary. There are many more books, and the school librarian (or the children's librarian in the local library) can help you with your choices.

The key elements to look for are animals and adventure, preferably fantasy. You can also ask various children in your class to recommend books they have especially enjoyed, and you can skim them at home to see if the class at large would enjoy them. If you sense that the majority of your students are bored or uninterested with a book for you are reading, don't feel hurt and rejected. Just find another book. Remember that you want your pupils to enjoy the experience of listening to stories. Short fairy tales and legends are great to fill in these 15 minutes we were just discussing.

WOULDN'T YOU LIKE TO SEE MY ETCHINGS?

Sharing your hobbies with your children is a very good way to establish rapport or for filling in 15 minute gaps in the school day. It is also a good way to get your feelings hurt, resulting in your harboring a bitter thought or two. Most adults eventually learn that most people couldn't care less about anybody's hobby but their own, and are hardly capable of feigning polite interest for more than 10 minutes.

You may, howevever, have a hobby that could prove of educational interest to your students. Most children are somewhat intrigued by collections (coin, stamp, models, butterflies), sports equipment, or artsy-craftsy hobbies. They are more interested in the latter if you let them try their hand.

One thing to be said for increase in the number of male elementary school teachers is that many of them have very useful hobbies that can add spice and excitement to their curricula. I have known several men teachers who were interested in photography, skin diving, oceanography, "ham" radio, electronics, and printing. You can see the great possibilities in incorporating such skills and talents into one's program. Women, unfortunately, either don't have hobbies or tend have one that only interest other females, such as sewing, embroidery, crocheting, or collecting antique china. Cooking is the one exception, and boys seem even more enthusiastic about this hobby than girls.

FOCUS ON LEARNING CENTERS

The learning, interest, or activity center is fast becoming a feature in classrooms all over the United States. Like most innovations, it is more prevalent in and around urban areas. The learning center can be used in many ways in a classroom. Children can go to it as a free time activity when they have finished their regular assignments. The center can be keyed to a particular subject area, like a science center or a math center, or it can be geared to a particular activity that the teacher wishes children to become involved in, like a food chemistry center where the task is to test various foods for different nutrients. The centers can be part of your regular instructional program and not merely for the use of students whose work is completed. Many school program their pupils into various learning centers each day as part of the course of studies.

Learning centers provide an ideal outlet into which you can plug in your gifted children or rapid workers who finish large group assignments early. Just be sure, when you select activities for a center, to have them cover a range of difficulty, in order that there will be something to challenge even the brightest students.

Two types of learning centers that teachers have found useful are static subject centers and specific skill centers. Static centers have a longer life and are concerned with the general aspects of the subject. Specific skill centers, as the term indicates, focus on specific skills, like the use of the comma, and should be changed whenever you move on to a new topic. Although centers involve a lot of work, they are interesting and challenging for the teacher as well as the student. Here is a chance to discover how creative you are! For a start, let me suggest a few ideas.

A static math center can be stocked with geo-boards; flash cards dealing with addition, subtraction, multiplication, division, or fractions, depending on the grade level; math concentration games; math bingo games; or geometry games, like matching shapes. Educational supply houses and toy shops usually are good sources of math games. If your budget is limited, you can make many of them yourself. Be sure to have handmade games laminated in plastic, or they will self-destruct in a few days. A tape-player or a record player can also be set up with arithmetic fact-drill tapes or records. I find it a good idea not to put out all my games at the start of the term. Instead, I hold back about half of them and replace them, one at a time, from my reserve supply. This keeps the children coming back to the center every few days to see whether anything new has been added.

The math puzzle center is actually a bulletin board. Ditto off 10 successively difficult word problems, the more bizarre and convoluted the better. The first problem should be fairly simple, and none of the problems should involve mathematical operations beyond the level of your students. If you include the names of the children in your class in the problems, the interest value will be greatly increased. Make the problems humorous, too. Make 10 envelopes to hold the dittos and staple them to the bulletin board. Next to each envelope, pin a card (face down) with the answer to the problem written on it. The idea of this task is to have each child fill his extra time with challenging and tantalizing mental exercise. Encourage the children not to peek, but to attempt the problem and attack it in several different ways before looking at the answer. You should have the children show their computations on the ditto, in order to get credit for having worked the problem. You might award "Mathematical Master" certificates to those students who complete the whole series of 10. Make copying another's work difficult.

Static Science Centers are the absolute worst to set up and maintain, next to art centers. I have yet to see a static type of science center, and the only good ones I know of are geared to a specific science activity. It takes a lot of fooling around and a lot of money to get a good science learning activity off the ground. Many books of "easy" science experiments will tell you as one of their selling points that they make use of readily available materials that you can find at home. I don't know about you, but I never happen to have bottles of limewater or phenolphthalein solution lying around my house. If you make a really diligent search, however, you should be able to come up with several experiments, that will satisfy the following criteria: 1. The materials to be used really are inexpensive and readily available. Preferably, the children can bring them from home, but don't count on it. 2. The experiment is fairly hazard-free, and no child will run the risk of being incinerated, poisoned, or blinded. 3. The experiment must be simple, and your directions can therefore be easily followed.

There is hardly much point in setting up a learning center that must be supervised by you. Learning centers are supposed to free the teacher to work with those youngsters who need special help, and at the same time to help children learn to follow direction on their own.

Another source of ideas for science centers are the classroom laboratories that often come with science textbooks. Many of these kits have accompanying booklets that describe simple experiments that children at that grade level can carry through by themselves. Another good science center idea for upper graders is a chemistry set. I got mine with Blue Chip Stamps, and it was a godsend, except when one little boy drank some phenolphthalein solution on a dare. (He was all right after the school nurse made him vomit.) You should go through the lab manuals that accompany these sets, and copy out some of the experiments onto large pieces of colored tagboard. Simplify the language while you're at it, since most authors of books of instruction that go with children's chemistry sets seem to assume that all young users are reading on the twelfth-grade level. You run into things like, "Prepare a dilute solution of sodium chloride," instead of, "Put some salt in water."

TWO SCIENCE CENTERS

Color Fun. This center developed from a lesson taught by one of my students on mixing colors. If possible, set this center up under a wall area where you can put up a bulletin board. Display a colorful and stimulating bulletin board on color and light. For the primary grades, you could use a large figure of a clown or an Easter bunny surrounding by buckets of paint. For the upper grades, maybe an elephant or the figure of a housepainter dressed in overalls could be used. The core of the center is a taped lesson with accompanying ditto on how various colors are mixed to get new ones. You can bring in the concepts of saturated hues, tones and shades, and primary and secondary colors, contrasting colors, and be as technical and scientific as you wish. While the children are listening to you on the tape, they are actually doing what you are talking about by coloring the dittoed sheets you have provided. Supplementary activities at the center could be color problems to be solved; some experiments with a prism, if you have one available, would also reinforce the concept. Some tempera paints for a bit of careful mixing might be interesting, too.

Be A Food Detective! A bulletin board depicting a bloodhound sniffing at footprints, on which are written, "Be a Food Detective! Follow the directions on the cards," forms the background and the general directions for this center. The laminated cards below on a table give directions on how to test foods to determine the presence of various nutrients. The instructions are too lengthy to repeat, but most science books for teachers give the directions. One of the easiest is a standard test for the presence of starch that most people are familiar with—all you need is a bottle of iodine. Drip a drop of iodine on the food and it will turn blue if starch is present. There are also tests for proteins and minerals. Include a chart where students can fill in what foods they tested and what the results were. Another similar center that you can set up involves discovering the solubility of different solids in water and other liquids. Children can attempt to dissolve cinnamon, sugar, salt, pepper, flour, and other things in water and record their results.

STATIC READING CENTERS

There is no dearth of phonics games on the market, and a few, chosen carefully to reflect the needs of your students, will be very useful items. Many of these games can be copied, but so many are surprisingly inexpensive that it is not worth your while to make them yourself. I have sent lots of business to our local educational supply shop, for parents are always asking me to recommend something to help their child with reading. I drag out a few trusty phonics games to show them and tell them where they can be purchased. There is something exciting for most children in being able to have at home the same game you have played with at school.

LEARNING CENTERS AD LIB.

1. Creative writing. Poetry, stories, writing from laminated photographs, and making your own books. Writing to music on a tape recorder is an interesting twist.
2. Arts and Crafts. Easel painting, craft projects, clay, and paper projects. Any self-directing activity that doesn't need teacher supervision or assistance is good for an art center.
3. Construction center. This has been recommended for use in classes for the emotionally handicapped. Building and creating with woods and tools is fascinating especially for boys. I saw one film in which a construction center featured a complete set of plumbing equipment, donated by a child's father.
4. Animals. Children like all kinds of animals, and classroom pets can be used for all kinds of learning. Petting or holding an animal for a specified period of time could be a reward for performing a certain activity, or children could do research on the animals. Rats, guinea pigs, snakes, birds, and fish are good pets. I would select rats and guinea pigs over all the others, since they are soft and furry, easy to care for and clean up after, and have easily met food needs. Rats are intelligent and guinea pigs are stupid, so whatever trait you appreciate, select your classroom pet on that basis. I have had poor luck with rabbits, including the Miniature Dutch variety, because the presence of too many people frightens them, and they become skittish and ill-tempered.
5. Library centers were around, even when I was in elementary school. A comfortable corner with a rocking chair or an easy

chair in a pleasant oasis of tranquillity in a busy classroom. One teacher I know has a fake fur rug, which makes the center a popular nook for his third graders to curl up in and enjoy their books. The *dernier cri* in library centers, which was used by another teacher at my school, and has been used in other nearby schools, is an old-fashioned, claw-footed bathtub, lined with a soft rug. The tub holds two readers at a time, sans shoes. In this second grade, even ordinarily reluctant readers plead with her for a chance to read in the bathtub.

6. Listening to stories on record or tapes is a good learning activity for students of all ages. Sometime you may want them to listen for sheer enjoyment or literary value—for example, to a record of *Treasure Island*—but usually there should be some sort of follow-up activity. Children should be listening for a purpose, not simply for entertainment. Too many teachers simply plug in their children to darling Walt Disney songs and forget about them for awhile, but the activity has no educational value unless the children are given something to look for or think about while they are listening. ("How would you spell supercalifragalisticexpealidocious?" you might ask the children before they listen to Mary Poppins music. "Could you use it in a sentence? What does Mary Poppins mean when she says this word?" Such teasers fall into the category of Critical Listening and Following Directions.)

7. Typing. Students with perceptual problems, especially dysgraphia, need access to typewriters, but all your other students will eventually need to learn typing as well. Many of my fourth-graders are already handing in typed reports, and I feel this is all to the good. I keep a typewriter in my classroom for use mainly in creative writing. It is a bribe to write stories, because once you have written an extra story, you are allowed to type it on the typewriter. I also let students use it for some of their classwork. If I hadn't learned to type in school, this book would never have seen the light of day. I certainly wouldn't have attempted it in my best Noble and Noble cursive schoolteacher handwriting!

12

¡ust for the record

The best advice is to be generous with your record keeping. You will always find yourself wishing you'd written down what you didn't. It is far better to keep extensive records than to keep cursory and incomplete ones, because you will absolutely without fail need to know a particular piece of information when you didn't record it. If you are only glad once or twice a year for nine months of scrupulously careful records, you have your just reward.

Every day for the first year I painstakingly wrote down the names of children who were absent on my desk calendar, wondering all the time why I was doing it. In May I found out. We were having a truancy problem with one boy, and his mother was trying to track this matter down. I was able to supply her with the exact dates her son had not come to school, which proved very helpful.

I also write down who is tardy and how many minutes he is late. If tardiness becomes a habit, I can then give the parents specific evidence like, "Martin was 10 minutes late for school on March 5th, 7th, and 8th." Many children are late for school simply to see if they can get away with it, but if a child gets caught every time by a careful teacher who writes everything down, it is not worth trying to get away with the act.

I keep many records mainly because I was so impressed with how much I was learning about the children from doing so. I keep attendance records in the manner I mentioned above. This makes it easy for me to fill out the computer printout sheet that my school requires for district records.

I also keep a composition-sized notebook on my telephone stand at home in which there is a page for every child, headed up with his full name, address, and telephone number, his parents' names, and their business address and profession. I also record the child's birthdate, his IQ score, and the name and ages of his siblings. Whenever I need to call his parents at home, I just pull out this book to find the phone number. I keep a written record of every phone call, with the date, time, and what was covered in the conversation. This is a very useful device, and it is certainly worth the time it takes to collect this data on every child in your room. At school, in the far corner of my desk drawer, I keep any anecdotal record cards that I might be using to keep notes on chronic behavior offenders.

If your school doesn't supply each teacher with a decent grade book, buy one. There is never enough room in the back of lesson plan books to record grades properly. I try to record a couple of grades each week for each child in the academic subjects. I include not only tests but also daily assignments of different types, so I can get a profile of each child's work habits at a quick glance. For example, the entry depicted here (Figure 12) tells me that after two months of school Jodi Carlson thrives on open-ended creative writing assignments, but is weak in straight grammar work, especially that involving verbs.

(*Figure 12*). Sample entry from a grade book.

For each grade, I write down what the assignment was, and how many it was possible to get right. It doesn't do any good to record student test scores carefully only to discover at report-card time that you can't recall how many total points there were on that particular test. Very annoying.

DIFFERENT STROKES FOR DIFFERENT FOLKS

Some teachers feel that grades should not be given and, when they required to do so, rate all children high, regardless of what progress they are making, thereby subtly sabotaging the system. My feeling about grade is that evaluation is an inescapable part of every social situation. Two people engaged in a casual conversation, for example, cannot escape evaluating each other and their own behavior as well. The fact that they are unaware of doing this does not make the evaluation any the less real. In school, evaluation goes on all the time among children and between teachers and children, even when the teacher does not record grades and indignantly denies any intention of doing so. How much more honest to record the grades and let the children know how they are doing!

Furthermore, I doubt whether any really significant learning occurs without some kind of feedback. If a learner doesn't know how he is doing, how can he correct himself and make necessary adjustments in this efforts?

The individualized reading program that I have been using requires me to keep a conference notebook in which I write down comments each time I have a personal conference with a child. In addition to this notebook, I keep a reading skills card on every child in the class. This card is my running record of what skills a child lacks, which ones he has mastered, which ones need to be re-presented, and any disturbing or gratifying trends that I notice. You will find such cards helpful in your conferences with the parents of a child who is having reading problems. You can pinpoint for them the areas in which the child needs the most help and the areas in which he is already competent.

My final record is not for my use but for the children's, and it is a list of who has held what monitorships, who was chosen as "Citizen of the Week" (or Month), and who has been team captain during physical education. You cannot imagine how many heated arguments can erupt over such vital issues as, "You were *so* art monitor before!" or "Ynez *always* gets picked for Citizen of the Week!" You can produce written proof that Daniel was definitely art monitor last November, and there have been several other Citizens of the Week besides Ynez.

CUMULATIVE RECORDS: TO CUM OR NOT TO CUM

Some of the data you will be collecting about a child will end up in his cumulative record, often called a "cum" (pronounced "cume") by teachers. A child's cumulative record is a large filing folder in which all sorts of essential and trivial items are kept. This record follows the child throughout his elementary school career and, in some school systems, it is retained through senior high school. In the cum, there are blanks or forms where every teacher is required to write informative comments about the child's leadership potential, intellectual ability, interests, home life, and anything else that seems relevant. There are usually entries and blanks for standardized test scores, grades, and attendance records, as well as reports of parent-teacher conferences.

There is considerable debate in the public schools over whether a teacher should read the cums before school begins in September, or should wait until much later in the year. Some skeptics claim they never read them at all, until they make their own entries in June.

Here are some arguments favoring the thorough study of each child's cum before you see him on the first day of school. Reading the cums before school opens gives you some idea of what kind of class you are likely to have. This assumes that you have a class list (otherwise, you don't know whose cums to read, anyway), and that you can lay your hands on the cums of all your prospective students, or at least the cums of those children who attended your school last year. The records of your transfer students will not be available until their former school sends them, which may sometime be after the spring thaw. Before you weed through all the printed matter inside the cum, have some idea of what you wish to find out about your new students. Here is some information to look for.

1. Intelligence test scores or IQs. Although these by no means tell the whole story about a child and may understate potentialities, they do provide a rough index to the amount of difficulty a child will have in learning. Children with 115 to 120 IQ and more are often the ones who finish their work early and need to have something else lined up for them. Those with IQs in the 80s and lower are likely to need special help, particularly during the first few weeks of school. Be on the alert for marked variations in the IQs of children who have been tested more than once. In general, the highest of several IQs is more representative of a child's potential. The idea is that a child cannot accidentally get a high IQ, but he can accidentally (because of emotional stress or misunderstanding directions) get one that is too low.

2. Achievement test data. See if any of your students have particularly high or low scores in any of the subject areas covered on the test.

3. Grades from last year. Look for unusual patterns, like a child who gets all As and a D in physical education, or the other way around. Or a child who had Cs in everything but science and math, in which he got As. Facts such as these are of great value in helping a child through the beginning of a new school year. If you know what he likes or does well in, you can capitalize on it during these first few weeks. If you know by a child's grades from last year that he is a top math student, you might want to enlist his help in setting up a math game table, for example.

4. The comments of previous teachers. At best, these comments are likely to be somewhat cryptic and give you only a glimpse of what the child is truly like. Hopefully, you may gain some insight into the child's home situation that can assist

you in understanding him before you really get to know him. Look for comments like, "divorce in family this year," "parents did not come to conferences," "father deserted family this year, "new baby born this year," and other revealing remarks. Last year's teacher may have listed some of the child's special interests or skills, such as athletic ability (or lack of it), artistic talent, or musical skills. All these are useful items to know.

5. The child's reading level or last reader completed as of the previous June. This is extremely helpful in forming reading groups. If you are using state-prescribed basal readers, you will probably wish your students to move forward in the official sequence by assigning the next book on the master list. You need to know who will be ready for which book and, from this information, you can form your groups fairly accurately.

If you are using an individualized program, you want to know the child's instructional level so you can have the appropriate materials ready for him. You may wish to do your own reading testing during the first month of school, but information from last year can help you to get the ball rolling in the right direction. All this information can help you formulate a kind of "class profile" in your mind.

6. Look for evidence of behavior problems or children who have trouble getting along with some particular youngsters who are also to be in your room. When you plan your seating arrangement for the first day, you will thus know in advance who should be separated from whom, and who needs to be somewhat isolated to prevent difficult situations from erupting during the first days of the new semester. If Alfonso Hidalgo had problems with controlling his talking last year, you will be doing him a great service if you seat him next to an empty desk on the first day instead of placing him right in the thick of things, surrounded by temptation.

Now we will hear the arguments favoring the postponement of looking at the cums until one gets to know the youngsters. The most telling point is that it is very easy to prejudice yourself against a particular child by reading the not-too-favorable remarks written by previous teachers. Some school systems allow teachers to pull out the stops when filling in the cums, and you may encounter comments like these: "Alfonso has a tendency to shout out in class. He is a constant talker, interrupts his classmates and teacher frequently, and throws things. He has a negative and extremely hostile attitude about school and authority figures in general." If you encounter remarks like these in enough folders, you may consider resigning before school opens or at least requesting another class, but don't let them scare you. Nevertheless, a comment like this will lead you to be apprehensive about Alfonso. You may subconsciously expect trouble from this young man, and he who anticipates trouble usually gets it. Alfonso now has a reputation of being a Bad Apple before he has even entered the classroom door. Therefore, you may find yourself jumping all over Alfonso the first time he says something without raising his hand, whereas you would ignore the same behavior in someone else who doesn't have his reputation. It is always possible, too, that Alfonso has determined to turn over a new leaf this year and comes to his new teacher prepared to make a fresh start. If you didn't know about Alfonso's behavior last year, you would probably give him at least an even break.

A second point in favor of postponing the reading of cums is that a teacher's comments are likely to reveal as much (and sometimes more) about the person who wrote them than they do about the child in question. A review of the comments written by the same teacher the children in her class may show, for example, that she values art skills more than reading and math skills, that she is unconcerned about disruptive behavior, and that she is only interested in a child's creativity. Another teacher may be preoccupied with conduct problems; still another may like boys but be prejudiced against girls (although it is usually the other way around). It is better to reserve judgment until you get to know the teacher who wrote the comments. In this instance, "getting to know" implies more than a "Good morning, how are you?" relationship and includes observing how the teacher interacts with children—on the playground, for example. Most teachers are delighted to share their philosophy of education with you, and it shouldn't take much prompting on your part to find out what viewpoints lie behind those cryptic but tantalizing notes in the cums of their former students.

Still another argument is that postponing the reading of cums leaves you free to make independent judgments about your children. Children's personalities often are in states of flux and may change from year to year, sometimes drastically. Last year's Little Angel may be this year's troublemaker, and last year's slow math student may suddenly catch fire with multiplication this year. A teacher's impression of a child depends partly on the teacher's own personality, so that the child who drove Mrs. Smith right up the wall in second grade may be one of the nicest kids in your third-grade class. Conversely, the child who worshipped Miss McRae in the fifth grade, may not feel so warmly towards his new sixth-grade teacher. It is a worthwhile exercise in professionalism to size up each of your new students as *you* see them. Let yourself discover who is artistic, musically inclined, or outstanding in spelling. See for yourself who works quietly, talks constantly, or fights on the playground. Then pull out the cums after a couple of months of school and see what you find. You may be very surprised in some cases. Another thing to keep in mind is that IQ scores and grades from last year may not be a very good indication of how well a child will perform this year. As he encounters new and more challenging work in a higher grade, he may run into difficulty, or he may suddenly begin to catch on as he never did before.

Although IQs can be helpful in a crude, approximate kind of way, they can also be misleading. One year I had a student whose IQ in third grade was 106. I had read the cums before school began and, consequently, was pleasantly surprised when this child turned in very superior work. It became obvious to me, as the year wore on, that this boy was capable of extremely complex inductive and deductive reasoning. He also was whizzing through the fourth-grade readers with almost perfect comprehension. In the spring, when I was asked to recommend students for testing for the school district's mentally gifted program, I submitted this child's name along with six others. He was the only member of my class who qualified overwhelmingly for the program, with an IQ of 137. Only two other fourth-graders were accepted into the program. I never found out why his third-grade score was so low; it could have been due to any number of factors or conditions. Had I not read this boy's cum before I had gotten to know him as a student, he would not have had to convince me that he really was as bright as he is. I would have accepted him at face value right from the start.

The opposite experience also occurs: the child with a high IQ can do badly. When this occurs, there is a tendency to put him under more pressure than the average student receives: "I *know* you can do better; I don't think you're *really trying*."

The reasons for the poor performance are usually psychological—for instance, the child relates to and does well on a printed, cut-and-dried test but falls apart when teachers ask him to do what every other child is doing. Putting direct pressure on the child may only aggravate whatever problem he happens to have.

I don't have any pat formula for dealing with such children—I just try to take them as they come and to understand them on their own terms. My only point here is that knowing a child's IQ may lead you to deal with him in ways that are inappropriate to his situation.

Conclusion: Should a teacher see the cums whenever she has the urge to do so? After considering the pros and cons, I feel it is a matter of personal taste and style. In other words, she should decide for herself. I cannot defend a binding principle where cums are concerned.

13

getting over wanting them to love you

There are two kinds of people: those who say that love makes the world go around, and those who say that it is money. I wouldn't know about the second—everyone I know seems to work harder for love than for money. This is hardly surprising, since love is a universal need. Everyone hopes to be liked, accepted, and respected by the people he knows and particularly by those with whom he lives and works, and teachers are no exception.

ON BEING LIKED AND OTHER MANY-SPLENDORED THINGS

As a matter of fact, being favorably regarded by others is a crucial factor in teachers' work. A teacher wants to be liked and accepted by his principal and his fellow teachers, but most of all, he desires acceptance and friendship from the people with whom he works the most closely—his pupils. As I will point out, liking and acceptance are not the same as love, although many beginning teachers confuse them.

Many student teachers are overwhelmed at first by the acceptance and interest displayed by the students. "Wow," they think, "These kids really like me! They're always talking to me, confiding in me, and wanting to walk with me on the playground. I'm really somebody to them."

I remember my surprise at the high degree of interest that my sixth-grade pupils showed in all my doings when I was their student teacher. It was almost like being the most popular child in an elementary school class. Before I even got up to teach my first lesson, children had fought to sit next to me, to carry my books, and to hang up my coat. The girls complimented my clothes, my jewelry, my hair, and my fingernail polish. They wanted to know my birthday, my favorite color, my favorite movie star, and if I had any animals. The boys were interested in me also, and asked what my husband did, if he liked sports, and when I told them he rode a motorcycle, they were my friends for life.

Having been so overwhelmed with supportive interest in the beginning, I naturally wanted to escalate my relations with these children and to have them love me as well. I didn't realize, as I later discovered, that *every* student teacher who is not shy or standoffish receives similar treatment. Children consider a student teacher to be their own personal property. A student teacher is usually young and friendly and is considered to be a pal. My problems began when I subsequently viewed any misbehavior on these students' part as a personal act of unfriendliness toward me!

"What's the matter with Steve?" I despaired, "I thought he liked me. Why is he doing this to *me*?"

What I didn't realize was once the initial excitement wears off, and as the student teacher takes over more responsibility from the master teacher, he becomes part of the classroom ménage and is treated more like other teachers. At this point, the students will begin to play some of the same games I have mentioned in earlier chapters. After a few disturbing disappointments, followed by a couple of serious talks with my master teacher, I began to realize what I *really* wanted from the children. What I *had* been wanting was love, but now I realized that whatever love they could give me was not only insubstantial and not very dependable but that it actually *interfered* with our relationship.

I came to the conclusion that I did want children to like me, but that my hopes and expectations were modest. All that was necessary was for them to like me well enough to accept me as a person who was going to direct their learning. I wanted their respect and their obedience, as well. But I really didn't want them as *friends*, in the full sense of the word. I wanted to be *friendly* to them, and wanted them to behave in a *friendly* manner towards me, but I really didn't want to be "bosom buddies" with them. I wanted to be a nice *teacher*, not a nice *pal*.

No matter how much a child likes you as a person, he never forgets that you are top dog. When it comes down to the line, it is you, the teacher, who has the last word. Teachers who try too hard to be buddies with their pupils are going to have difficulty getting that last word when they need to have it. This is more of a problem in the upper elementary grades and junior high school than in the primary and middle grades. For one thing, older children are more like adults, and it is easier to overlook the age-and-maturity gap. For another, children in the preadolescent and adolescent years are more likely to develop a "crush" on a teacher, and it is hard for a teacher to avoid being flattered by the extra attention he is receiving.

Most teachers (if only it were *all* of them!) like children, or they would not be in the teaching profession, and it is natural for them to seek and encourage indications of positive feeling and to reciprocate in kind. The fact that a teacher wants his relationship with his pupils to be on a friendly basis does not mean that he should behave like a child or an adolescent or adopt their way of speaking. Children are never taken in by this, no matter how sincere the intentions of the teacher. Teachers (and I have known several) who are always trying to prove to their students that they are hip, will find their authority and stature greatly diminished in the eyes of their students. You do not have to behave like a maiden aunt to gain children's respect, but you do need to act like a responsible adult.

When I was student teaching in the sixth grade, the students (at the instigation of my master teacher) gave me a gala birthday party. I was the pampered guest of honor. There were flowers, cards, gifts, a birthday cake, and punch. I was very touched and flattered by being the center of all this attention.

I am afraid my head was a bit turned by this experience, because I rather expected and hoped that my fourth-graders during my first year of teaching would make this elegant gesture, too. I am embarrassed to say that I was a little hurt when they didn't. I think one child asked me, "Today is your birthday, isn't it, teacher?"

After I thought about the matter, I realized that I was really being childish to have expected anything at all. I *had* the respect of every child in my class. They were polite and kind to me every day of the year. They were learning and growing under my guidance and I was respected and liked by their parents as well. All these things were certainly worth more to me as a professional than a birthday party. I was glad to be liked and respected rather than loved and taken advantage of. Satisfaction comes from a job well-done. A teacher cannot afford to be childish and immature, and worrying over being Miss Popularity or Mr. Well-Beloved *is* childish and immature.

I will always remember a remark made to me on the playground by a slow-learning child. We were talking about Mr. Smith, a teacher in his final year before retirement.

"I like him," the boy said. "He's strict but nice, and you can really learn in his class. He's always ready to help you."

This kind of appraisal is worth much more than: "Gee, Mr. Jones is *so* cool. He brought all his rock records to class and lets us play them during English."

I may be letting my biases show when I say that there is a note of disappointment in comments like the latter. I sense that when a child says that he adores his teacher because he can get away with anything in his class, he is also saying that he wishes his teacher were mature enough to take control.

CLASSROOM STARS, OR THE TEACHER'S PETS

In normal classrooms, some children succeed more than others and, as a consequence, get rewarded or praised more than others. It is also inevitable that some children like their teacher more than others, and are liked in return. Whether it is by accident or design, in other words, every teacher has his favorites.

Now that we have admitted that liking some children more than others is normal we must, at the same time, say that displaying this special liking is dangerous. One of the unwritten laws of teacher behavior is: "Thou shalt not make a teacher's pet out of any child."

Every beginning teacher knows full well that having pets is dangerous and unhealthy. Children deeply resent favoritism, sometimes when they are the target of it and especially, of course, when they are not. A child who is obviously the class "star" is in a very precarious position when it comes to peer acceptance. His classmates tend to attribute his every success to the fact that the teacher likes him best. "Sandy always gets an A. She's the teacher's pet." The rest of the class feels very left out when one or two children are almost always chosen for choise monitorships or special coveted tasks. You already know that such behavior on a teacher's part breeds mutiny in a classroom.

It is easy to be careless about this, however, and to be unaware of showing favoritism. This is natural because in each classroom there are always a couple of students on whom you can really depend, and you tend to choose them over the others when something complex or special arises. You can always trust such youngsters to be on their best behavior when a visitor comes to your room, so naturally you pick them to give a guided tour or set up chairs and explain the assignments in progress.

Everyone has a tendency to want to show off their best pupils. I learned my lesson but good during student teaching when our class had two VIP visitors from the Orient. The whole class had been primed and prepared for their visit, and who did I naively choose for the coveted job of personal host for the guests? That's right—Ted, the boy who had everything, whom everyone dearly loved, especially me. Ted was a paragon: he had brains, looks, athletic ability, and was quite an accomplished artist. He had a darling little sister, two delightful and warm parents, and was considered the best-dressed boy in the sixth grade. There was probably no child in that classroom who less needed the honor of official guide. I was laboring under the delusion that virtue needed to be rewarded, and I also wished our visitors to meet the cream of the sixth-grade crop. What I had not been aware of was that while the class admired and liked Ted, they were also jealous of him. The visitors had not been in the classroom more than 15 minutes when it became evident that anarchy was imminent. The others in the class were most disgruntled by my selection of this child, and it was necessary to change guides in midstream and appoint a series of hosts in order to salvage the situation. It worked out quite well, as it turned out, since no fewer than eight children got the chance to talk with the guests personally and escort them around.

The result of this and similar misadventures was that I became more sensitive to the needs of my students, and I became aware of my tendencies toward favoritism. Whether or not you suspect that you are succumbing to the practice of playing favorites, you should occasionally stop and analyze what you are actually doing. Perhaps you could write down on scratch paper the name of each child you choose to perform a special duty. Do this for about a week. If the same names keep cropping up again and again, you need to share the wealth a bit more. Try selecting as many different children as you possibly can to run errands, carry things, or assume special tasks. Many teachers select the brightest pupils to serve as messengers, on the grounds that only these children can afford to spare time away from their lessons and studies. This really isn't true. Children of average and lesser ability often need a break from routine more than their brighter classmates, and it does wonderful things for their less-than-adequate self-concepts if they are allowed to be messengers. Granted, these children sometimes get the message confused, but they usually improve with practice. Besides, if the message if really important, by all means write it down, rather than relying on word of mouth.

YOU DON'T HAVE TO LIKE THEM ALL

Again, it is inevitable that you will find that some children are more frustrating, obnoxious, or otherwise objectionable than others. Again, the teacher who is trying to play her professional roles in ways that are fair and unflappable, cannot afford to add to the problems that such children usually have by making her personal feelings evident.

But such children pose another problem, however. They

make us feel guilty. Somewhere in the unwritten code there seems to be the precept that a teacher should like—nay, *love* —all her children. Such precepts do not apparently apply to occupations other than those in the "helping" professions. Accountants and salespeople feel no twinges of guilt if they find that some of their clients evoke negative feelings. They are inclined to accept this discovery as an inevitable and unavoidable part of life. The tendency to feel guilt about disliking others seems especially characteristic of people in professions like teaching and counseling.

If you are particularly prone to such feelings, your first reaction to the discovery that a child's behavior annoys you is either that of blaming yourself or something other than the child.

"I should have waited instead of stopping Lisa from pouring the paint down the sink," you say.

"I shouldn't have taken John's book from Lisa," you say to yourself. "She would have found out quickly enough that it wasn't her book."

Or, "Lisa was looking rather droopy today. She probably doesn't get enough sleep, and this makes her irritable. I should have noticed that before I spoke to her."

There is nothing wrong with these insights, because they show that you are thinking about your own motives and other background elements that are important for understanding what goes on in the classroom. But if you continually find that you are blaming yourself and/or making excuses for having to speak to Lisa, you should face the possibility that you do not like her. She may not like you either, of course, in which event it is possible that her dislike is touched off or at least reinforced by your dislike for her.

Once you have come to face the probability that you do not like a child, put the lid on the guilt feelings that are now welling up within you more strongly than ever. Teachers and students are both human, and no human being can realistically expect to feel the same degree of liking for every single other human being. Bear in mind, also, that no matter how charming and delightful children can be, they can be equally annoying and obnoxious. It is also possible to be a very effective teacher for a child you dislike, so don't feel that your personal reaction is going to get in the way of doing a professional and competent job. The next step is to discover exactly what there is about this child that annoys you. Is it the way he says things? Is it his attitude toward authority or other children? Is it the fact that he is constantly demanding attention from you? Is it his slapdash work habits or his I-don't-care-attitude? I am assuming that you will not dislike a child on purely physical grounds, such as his color or appearance, so your reaction must be caused by his personality or behavior. Once you have found the cause of your feelings, you can begin to plan your approach.

One technique you can use with a child you do not like is to try to avoid encountering him in the situations where he is at his worst. Try not to let him involve you or trap you into situations in which there is any danger of your revealing negative feelings about him. Try to deal with this child when you are relaxed and unruffled and can give him your full attention. Such playing hard-to-get will often cut unpleasant encounters down to a minimum.

I am thinking of a child in my class one year who had a penchant for asking nosy and embarrassing questions about personal matters. He also tended to be a long-winded raconteur when he was called on in the middle of a lesson. Fortunately, this child had a way of tipping me off whenever he was disposed to embark on one of his convoluted and extraneous digressions. He would wave his hand wildly in the air when I asked for the correct spelling of "December" for example. I would call on him, and he would promptly settle back in his chair, and say, "This doesn't have anything to do with spelling, but . . ." at which point I would interrupt by saying, "Let's talk about that at another time, shall we? Right now we need to know how to spell December."

If he was somehow able to get started on his little spiel, I would cut him off politely by telling him, "I'm afraid we won't have time to hear all of what you are telling us now. Why don't you tell me the rest of it on the playground this afternoon?"

Nine times out of ten he forgot all about his fascinating story by afternoon recess time, and I was spared the juicy details. I handled his nosy questions in several ways. One was pretending not to hear him, while rapidly walking in the opposite direction. If he succeeded in trapping me, however, I put him off by saying, "I really don't know the answer to that question" or, if it was obvious that I must know the answer (e.g., "Why don't you and Mr. Fisk have any children?"), I said, "You really don't need to know that, Karl." This usually stopped him in his tracks, but every once in a while he would encounter with, "But I want to know anyway!"

"Well, Karl, you're not going to know, so just put it out of your mind."

I never said, although I would have loved to, "Why don't you mind your own business, you little gossip?"

The best approach, however, is that of trying to find something likeable about the child. This may not be easy, but you should be able to come up with some trait that evokes positive feelings from you. Once you have discovered it, capitalize on it.

One girl in my class last year really rubbed me the wrong way. Jill was bossy and negative in her dealings with other children, and always gave me the impression that she felt I really didn't know what I was doing. She was a great sower of seeds of insecurity! Her one redeeming feature was that she loved to write stories and had a fairly decent imagination. I made the most of this. I tried to restrict my personal contacts with her to the subject of writing. I read every story she wrote, and praised her copiously on her efforts in the literary field. I let her know that I felt her interest in writing was great. We talked about ideas for plots and the use of descriptive words to liven up her stories. Somehow I conveyed the impression that she was a very special person in our class, because she wrote stories so eagerly and so often.

Jill responded favorably to this treatment, and her parents even told me how they appreciated my encouragement in her writing. Soon they began to read her stories, and they got involved with her writing, also. This pleased her very much.

Once I had capitalized on this aspect of her personality and won her trust and support, I could then begin to correct some of her failings, too. I wasn't completely successful in curing her bossiness and aggressive tendencies, but at least we had some good grounds on which we could communicate positively, which was much better than none at all. I used story writing as a means of removing her from many classroom situations in which she habitually got into arguments. When a fight or a name-calling session seemed imminent, I would remove her from the situation by suggesting that she work on a story or, if I had time, that she talk to me about whatever she was working on.

Another thing you can do with the child you dislike is to try to be as pleasant as possible with him, even if it kills you. I forced myself to be pleasant and supportive to this little girl whenever I could, so that I was able to play the heavy when it became necessary. This way, she resented my authority far less when the heavy arm of discipline and control was lowered than if I had been cool and barely cordial to her the rest of the time. I tried my best to reinforce her when she was being tractable, and I saved my fire for those situations when she was not. I made an effort to behave as if I really liked her most of the time. When I did have to discipline her, I tried to convey the impression that I still felt favorably toward her, but her behavior in that instance left something to be desired.

14

parents: friends, enemies, or allies?

No matter how able you are, and no matter how dearly beloved you are by your students, you are doomed to play second fiddle to a far more potent and effective pair of teachers: your students' parents.

To be sure, a child's parents may not be able to teach him reading and math as well as you can because, in skill-and-information subjects, a nonparent usually can be more effective than a parent. It is from a child's parents, however, that he learns his basic attitudes, work habits, and motives—the whole psychological apparatus that will determine how much success and what kind of success he will have in your classroom.

By the time most children are in elementary school, the main patterns of this motivational apparatus are formed, but there are still many chances for corrective adjustment and readjustment, all of which can proceed more successfully if both parents and teacher collaborate. Furthermore, school represents the child's first major adventure into life outside the home. Your role is to encourage him in this adventure and to help him learn some of the basic information, skills, and concepts he will need. Your success at this, again, will depend on what kind of support you are getting at home.

KEEPING THE CHANNELS OPEN

The essence of good parent relations is communication. Parents typically want to know how their child is doing in school, and unfortunately, report cards do not provide sufficient information for them to see how well or how poorly their youngster is doing. There are many ingenious methods that school systems use to give parents more information than a mere letter grade. For instance, one district in which I taught reported whether the child was above, below, or at grade level in his achievement and whether his effort was outstanding, limited, or satisfactory.

No matter how much information is on the report card, a parent typically wants to know more: In what ways is my child below grade level in reading? Is it a poor vocabulary, is he slow, or what? In what ways can I help him? And so forth. What do "grade level," "limited effort," and "satisfactory effort" mean?

The only way you can begin to clarify such ambiguities is to communicate with parents frequently and in detail. Educational terms and jargon that seem clear to you are often incomprehensible even to well-educated parents. This includes fairly self-explanatory terms such as "grade-level work." It is fine to say that a child is performing at the fifth-grade level in math, but what exactly, does this mean? What skills is a fifth-grader expected to master? Bear in mind that it is far better to overexplain than to send a parent away confused.

USING THE TELEPHONE

I have found that the following techniques are helpful in securing parental support and even appreciation. I make considerable use of the telephone. We've discussed the use of the phone call when a child has committed an act of extraordinary misbehavior, but it is also a good idea to call every child's parents two or three times during the year for the purpose of keeping them up to date on their child's progress. A phone call is definitely in order when a child has done something extremely well, or when he is improving in any subject. Many teachers believe that speaking approvingly to a child at the time of his triumph is sufficient, presuming that the news will automatically reach the parents. Not so, for most children are somewhat embarrassed to run home shouting their successes to all and sundry, especially when there are other children in the family who might seize the opportunity to tease them. Children who are average or below-average students also run the risk of their family's disbelief: "Are you sure she said your drawing was good?" It is therefore far better to let the parents hear the good news from the teacher himself. They will believe it when you say so.

You don't need to spend a great deal of time on such phone calls; 10 minutes will do, with 5 minutes beforehand spent in planning what you are going to say and 5 minutes to make the call. If you can't get in touch with the parents, and a babysitter or sibling answers the phone, leave a shortened version of your message. Otherwise, the entire family would be worrying about the nature of your call until you are able to reach them, and the child would no doubt be subjected to a cross-examination of what he did wrong that day in school!

An example of something to say is as follows: "Mr. Swenson, I just wanted to let you know that Peter is doing much better in reading recently. He's really trying his best, and I'm very proud of the good job he's doing. He still isn't quite ready for the second-grade reading book, but I'm sure if he keeps trying as he has been lately that he'll be ready to start it soon." Mr. Swenson may be at a loss for words, but he will thank you, and pass the happy news on to the rest of the family. Now he knows about where Peter stands, and he will be able to ask you at a conference (or ask Peter) if Peter is reading in the second-grade book yet. Mr. Swenson may have known already that his son was not a very good reader, but he may not have known how hard the child was trying to improve, or how close he really is to reading at his grade level.

Calling the parents to relate an incident is a good way of getting the child to share it with his family. Let's say that our friend Peter has tried very hard and has written a very charming story about a baby duck. You read the story, wrote enthusiastic comments on the paper, and told Peter how good it was. Perhaps he was encouraged to read his story out loud to his classmates, who enjoyed it also. Peter's comments at home might be something like, "Today I got to read a story to the class, and everybody clapped." He doesn't make it clear to his mother that he wrote the story, and that it was the first time this year that he was able to get more than three sentences down on paper. His mother may also have been preoccupied when Peter was relating this incident, and it might not occur to her to ask him to read to her. If you call that evening, however, and tell them about how pleased you were with Peter's baby duck story and suggest that Mrs. Swenson ask him to read it to her, she will certainly comply with your request. Peter will read his story, and his family will see your comments on the paper. They will also have heard the same praises from you personally. Peter's parents will begin to be involved in his school career a bit more, and may start asking him, "Did you write any stories today at school? What did you write about?" instead of "What happened today at school?" to which the child will reply, "Nothing."

INFORM EARLY AND OFTEN

If a child begins to fall down a bit in a subject, it is important to let his family know so that they won't be in for a shock at report card or test time. If you wait and bide your time, hoping the child will return to his former level of performance, the parents will call you asking, "Why didn't you let us know that Claudia was doing badly in math? She always did so well, and we were very surprised and disappointed with her grade."

If you had informed the parents as soon as Claudia started having problems, perhaps her parents wouldn't have done anything, but at least they would have seen which way the wind was blowing. Chances are that they would have tried to help her at home, if you had suggested this. Having the family help their youngster with his school work at home accomplishes several things. First, the extra practice and attention will probably benefit the child, and his work may improve as a result. Second, the parents get involved in the child's education, instead of feeling as though they send the child off to school every morning and welcome him home every afternoon without knowing what he is learning or doing there. Third, the parents may gain insight into the problems and difficulties of teaching when they are trying to do it themselves. This is a good way of making parents aware of what sort of learner their child is. If he has learning problems or a short attention span, his parents will become painfully aware of this when they see the youngster in a learning situation. They may begin to think, "Wow! It's not so easy to teach Claudia her multiplication tables! I've got to hand it to that teacher if she has to put up with all this fidgeting and daydreaming!"

What you are trying to convey to each parent by communicating with them is that you are personally and professionally interested in their child, and that you want to help him do as well as he can in school. Incidentally, you are letting the parents know that as far as their child is concerned, you are earning your salary. Don't count on Glenn to tell his mother that the teacher sits down with him and spends 15 minutes every morning drilling him on his vowel digraphs—tell Glenn's mother yourself.

The mother may be thinking, "Why doesn't that teacher teach my son to read better? That's what we send the boy to school for. All these taxes aren't doing a darn thing for my child!"

If you have talked with Glenn's mother, and mentioned how hard you are trying to help Glenn ("I have been working with him alone for 15 minutes every day on his phonics."), she may still be disgusted with Glenn's reading ability, but at least she realizes that you are making a special effort to help her son.

THE WRITTEN WORD

If you don't have time to call the parents, but still want to let them know about their child's progress, you can write a note. The note could be written at recess, or you can ask the child to stay a few minutes after school while you compose it. Be sure to let the child know its contents in general, or else the note might not reach home at all! If a child believes that his teacher is writing a "bad" letter, he may conveniently lose it on the way home. If you need to report learning difficulties or poor behavior, it is better to phone than to write, since telephoning allows you to explain the situation more fully.

Another good way of communicating with parents in general is to ditto a weekly or monthly letter addressed to all the parents of your children. In such letters, you can inform the families of the units you are covering and will be covering in the near future, the concepts you are teaching in the various subject areas, and any special events forthcoming, such as field trips, special guests, plays, or parties. You can also request supplies for art projects. It is true that your carefully composed letters may end up unread in some wastebaskets, but the majority of parents will read and approve. One letter I wrote brought sacks full of fabric scraps for puppets, and every request I have made has brought some kind of positive response.

A good technique to employ with these regular letters home is to write the letter simply and briefly, with instructions that it be read aloud by each child to his parents. This works very well in the primary grades. With upper graders, a good way of insuring that the letter will be hand-delivered and hopefully read by parents is to leave the salutation blank, and have each child fill in Dear Mr. and Mrs. Blank on his copy. If a student has taken the time to do this, he is more likely to remember to give the letter to his family.

PITFALLS AND BOOBY TRAPS

Every child is seen differently by his teacher and by his parents. As the child's teacher, you see him as one of 20 or 30 others, whose academic and social education as a total group is your responsibility. Even when you see a child as an individual, you are bound to judge and compare him to the others in the class, consciously or unconsciously.

A parent's resources are much more limited. The most he can do is to compare the child to his siblings (a comparison that is usually unfair either to the child or to the siblings), to other children the parent knows (usually a fairly limited contact with a very limited number), or with his memories of himself at the same age. The teacher, in other words, is more likely to have a detached, objective, and fairly realistic view of the child, whereas the parent's picture is much less complete.

The chief difference between parents' and teachers' perceptions, however, comes in the emotional investment the parent has made and will continue to make in the child and his fate. Children are literally and figuratively extensions of parental egos: when a child fails, it is the parents themselves who have failed, and when a child succeeds, the success is theirs as well.

The surest way to alienate parents is to ignore this special relationship. A child's misbehavior may be a headache to you, but to his parents it is a personal embarrassment. Avoid the implication that a child's poor behavior is the fault of his parents, even if you are certain that it is. When you discuss a child's behavior with his parents, concentrate on the behavior itself, rather than the causes. Ask the parents, "How can we help James change his behavior?" instead of, "Why is he acting this way?"

Another good way of alienating parents is to pretend that everything is going smoothly with their child when it is not. If you perpetrate such false impressions, it will be a far worse shock to the parents when you are faced with escalating misbehavior or learning problems that surpass the level of your capability to handle and, hence, have to recommend drastic measures.

The absolutely best way of making enemies of parents is to be continually unavailable or unhelpful when they take the initiative and try to contact you. Most parents will not call the school and try to reach you unless they feel an urgent need to do so. If you receive a message to phone a parent at your earliest convenience, don't put off making the return call. When a parent sends a note to you via his child, take time to reply the same day, if at all possible. If you don't do this, parents are likely to go over your head and call on the principal for assistance, complaining at the same time about your lack of interest in their child. You will then have to explain to the principal why you didn't call Mrs. Smith back. When you do finally call her, she will not be feeling very friendly towards you. She will have complained to her neighbors that she had to call the principal before she could get the teacher to talk to her! And thus, you will get the reputation of being cavalier and uninterested.

HOW TO SURVIVE PARENT CONFERENCES

Most school systems require parent-teacher conferences at least once during every school year, and every teacher is expected to make the effort to see each parent during this conference period. In the case of children with behavioral or learning problems, you will probably conduct several conferences during the year with their parents. You will get to know these parents very well.

The first step to take in arranging parent conferences is to set up a schedule. My school has forms to be sent home on which the teacher writes the day and time he wishes to hold the conference. The parent returns the note stating whether or not he is able to attend at that time. Since more and more mothers are holding jobs outside of the home, this system turns into an extended interchange of notes requesting different times for conferences. I found that it is much easier to make conference appointments by telephone in the evening when I could be fairly certain that the parents were home. During my telephone call, I was also able to explain that the conferences were for all parents, not just those who had "problem children." This alleviates a parent's fear that he is the only one in your classroom who has to have a conference. By phoning the home, I am able to discover which mothers work at what times, and which mothers have other commitments or babysitting problems. I also find out which parents are not interested in coming to a conference at all. During the parent conference period, I make myself available until 6:00 P.M. for parents who are employed and cannot come until after work. I am willing to do this once, but if the child in question continues to have serious problems that require several conferences throughout the year, subsequent conferences are held during business hours.

Now that you have set up your schedule, you will begin your preparation for the conference. Begin saving examples of each child's work in all the subject areas for at least two weeks prior to the conference. If parent conferences are held in conjunction with report-card distribution, fill out the report cards. Your school may require a parent conference summary sheet to be filled out in duplicate, one copy to be kept by the parent and the other for school files. Even if you are not required to fill out a summary of points covered at the conference, it is a good idea to do so, since it gives the parent something to refer to when he arrives home. As usually happens, only the child's mother will attend and, after her husband comes home in the evening, he will question her about what happened at her conference. "What did the teacher say?" he will ask. If she has a summary sheet written by you, all she has to do is to hand it to him to peruse instead of admitting that she can't remember what you told her.

Your copy of the conference report is also a useful tool in case of a continuing problem with a particular youngster. At later conferences you can refer to the first report and remark, "I see that we discussed Veronica's difficulties with getting her assignments done on time at our last conference."

Here's Sean Williams' mother at your classroom door, ready for her conference. You invite her in graciously, exchange pleasantries, and escort her to a table where you have his report card, conference summary sheet, and a folder filled with his papers. How do you begin? Start out positively, referring to the child's strengths first. Then move on to his problem areas and weaknesses. Sean is an extremely capable and intelligent third-grader, who tends to be pretty lazy about getting his work done. He is highly talkative and bothers everyone within a one-mile radius of his work area. He is doing adequate work in all subject areas, but you know he is capable of lots more. Here's how you handle this conference with Mrs. Williams.

Mrs. W: How's he doing?

You: Fairly well so far. Sean is a very intelligent child, and he is an excellent reader. He reads on about the fourth-grade level according to a reading test we gave him in September. He seems to catch on to everything very quickly.

Mrs. W: That's nice to hear. He was always bright when he was little, not like his younger brother in first grade. I feel sorry for *his* teacher. (Now you know that Sean is this mother's pride and joy. She already has problems with the younger child, and sort of counts on Sean to do well so she doesn't have to worry about him. You're going to have to tread softly.)

You: I think Sean is really capable of doing very high-quality work. He certainly has outstanding ability, and he comes up with some very intelligent answers during class discussions.

Mrs. W: Sean talks a blue streak at home. He's always chattering about something. With three other kids, I really don't have much time to listen to him a lot of the time. (Here's one reason why Sean is so talkative in class. Maybe he's trying to make up for the attention he isn't getting at home.)

You: Yes, he is a very talkative child. Sometimes I have to speak to him about talking at the wrong times during work periods. Often, he has a bit of a problem getting settled down after a discussion period is over. I think he needs to work on this a little, because he sometimes disturbs other children when we're trying to work quietly.

Mrs. W: (Apprehensively) Doesn't he do what he's told?

You: Most of the time he tries to, but he does have a problem in controlling his talking during class. He needs to be reminded about this often. Because of the talking, Sean sometimes has difficulty completing his assignments. (At this point you might show Mrs. Williams one of Sean's half-finished papers, emphasizing that what has been done is excellent, but unfortunately the paper wasn't finished.)

Mrs. W: I'm sorry to hear this. I thought he was doing well this year.

You: Sean is such a nice, friendly boy, and he really likes to share his thoughts with other children. He is very well liked and, when he makes an effort, he can do beautiful work. He just needs to try a little harder more often. How does he like school this year?

Mrs. W: He seems to like it fine, better than last year. At his other school, he got away with murder. The teacher didn't pay much attention to what was going on in that class. (Another reason for Sean's talking and poor work habits. He has had nine months of being able to get away with it.) His Dad wanted to put him in a parochial school, but I said let's give the public school another try. We like this school so far.

You: Let's see if we can't help Sean to make the most of his abilities. Fortunately, he doesn't have any trouble understanding or keeping up with the work, and he is really very bright. Maybe you or your husband could have a talk with him about the importance of finishing up his assignments and trying to control his talking.

Mrs. W: I'll certainly do that. We have to spend a lot of time controlling his little brother, but I'll see what I can do.

You: Good. I'll try to see that Sean brings home any unfinished assignments to do as homework, so he doesn't get behind. We don't want that to happen. I'd really like to see Sean do very well this year, he certainly has lots of potential. I'm sure, if we both help him, that he will be able to get his work done quietly. If you have a moment during the week, maybe you could talk with him alone about what he's doing in school. I know he'd love to share this with you. Maybe he might be able to help you with his little brother's reading.

Mrs. W: I will try to talk to him alone if I get the chance, but I don't like him to help Steven because he's so impatient with him. He can't understand why Steven doesn't catch on like *he* does.

You: I'm afraid my next appointment is waiting outside, so

we'll have to discuss this some more later on in the year. I'll be letting you know how he is doing in a couple of weeks.

Mrs. W: I'd really appreciate it if you could. Thank you very much, and I'll see what we can do at home.

You: Goodbye, Mrs. Williams. I'm certainly happy to have Sean in my class this year. I enjoy working with him.

She leaves, bearing the report card, conference summary, and Sean's folder, prepared to discuss the situation with her husband.

You have learned quite a bit from this brief conversation. You know that Sean is having some difficulty adjusting to a school situation in which there is more structure than his last class; that he is the brightest child in his family; that his younger brother is being compared unfavorably to Sean; that he is impatient with children of lesser ability; that his father does not think much of public schools, and that you and the public school system are on trial, so to speak; and that his mother has her hands full with three other children, preventing her from giving Sean much personal attention.

Mrs. Williams should know now that her son is bright and has no learning difficulties (for which she is doubly grateful, considering her other school-aged child), she is aware he has some problems in school but knows what they are, and she knows that the teacher likes her child and wants him to do well just as much as she does. A good conference all around!

15

problem parents, problem children

If you have followed the prescription for good parent relations that we have already discussed, you will undoubtedly be popular with parents. A good 75 percent of parent antipathy against the schools has some reasonable basis. Most sensible parents become enraged over incompetence, lack of discipline, harsh and cruel punishments, or when they believe that no effort has been made to help their child with his problems. And, when a child has learning or behavioral difficulties, the majority of parents do not expect the problem to be completely and immediately solved by the teacher.

There is a small percentage of parents, however, who are inclined to be unreasonable and who do not respond to the teacher's efforts to be open, honest, objective, and helpful. Such people seem to be dissatisfied no matter what the school tries to do for their child. If you have truly done all that you can to help their youngster, calling on the principal and specialists for assistance and support, there is little more that you can do. As my principal once said, there is a point at which the teacher or the principal has to determine who owns the problem. If you have made a concerted effort to help a child and his parents with little or no result, it is they who own the problem, and it is up to them to solve it. If a child has learning difficulties that are so severe that special individual help from the teacher and the district specialist is not adequate, the child's family is simply going to have to seek help elsewhere. They will have to turn to some outside agency for assistance, such as family counseling, a child psychologist, or even a special school.

If you have the misfortune of being confronted by an angry parent whose dissatisfaction seems unreasonable, present the problem to the principal. If they have an unrealistic grudge against the school in general which they are unloading on you, this is a case for the principal to deal with. Give him all pertinent facts, and let him take it from there. Often, when irate parents are forced to deal with the head of the school, they feel flustered and, subsequently, they begin to feel a bit foolish and may back off and forget about it.

Sometimes a teacher can make mistakes that set a parent off because the parent or the child has not provided the teacher with enough information to make a proper decision. During my first month of teaching, an angry mother called my principal complaining that I refused her daughter permission to go home for lunch. The child had gone to the office, and the school clerk had telephoned her family. By the time the mother was located at work, there was barely enough time for the girl to get home and eat her lunch before school began again in the afternoon.

What happened was that the girl had left her lunch money in her desk, and one of the children had taken it. When it came time for lunch, the class lined up and walked down to the cafeteria as usual. It was then that this young lady asked me if she could go home for lunch. I asked if she had a note from her mother since our school required written permission before a child can leave the school grounds to eat at home. She didn't have a note so I sent her to the office to see if the mother could give permission over the phone. The child never told me that she wanted to go home because her lunch money was stolen. Had she told me this, I would have given her enough money to buy lunch. The girl realized that she should have told me the reason for wanting to go home so she told her mother that her money was stolen and that the teacher wouldn't do anything about it. The whole situation could have been avoided if the child had been clear about her predicament in the first place.

IT'S ALL HIS FATHER'S FAULT

In this time of many divorces and family squabbles, an inexperienced teacher can be maneuvered into taking sides in marital disputes without realizing what is happening. Teachers should obviously be on guard against involvement in the family affairs of her students, if only because such involvement can be personally hazardous. Fathers threaten the lives of mothers, and one of my students lived in perpetual fear of being kidnapped at gun-point by his estranged father. Other scary family situations also occur without the word getting back to the school.

Family quarrels and problem behavior go hand in hand. The imminent breakup of a family is almost certain to precipitate some kind of school-related problem behavior: defiance, abject withdrawal, gross inattention, sudden regressions in skill subjects, and so forth. A child cannot live in an atmosphere characterized by violent argument, one or both parents leaving for extended periods of time, constant undercurrents of bickering, or disguised or open hostility without there being some kind of fallout in the form of a school problem. Inevitably you will be conducting conferences with the parents of these children who are chronic misbehavers. Inevitably, parents will take this opportunity to unload their marital difficulties on you. Once you have had Teddy's mother in to discuss his uncooperative behavior, you will probably find Teddy's father beating down your classroom door demanding equal time. He figures that Teddy's mother has made all kinds of outrageous accusations, and it is his privilege to set the record right. After a wearing session with the father you are likely to hear from Teddy's mother again, demanding the right of a rebuttal. Then back comes Teddy's father ready to do battle again. These parents will tell you far, far more than you want to know about the child's home situation and, if you are unable to nip this in the bud tactfully, you will be regaled with sordid accounts of sexual problems and unfaithful spouses.

THE TEACHER AS A NONTHERAPIST

Many people regard teachers and principals in the same light as clergymen, psychiatrists, and doctors and, therefore, feel free to spell out the clinical details of their most intimate problems. Although such faith and confidence is flattering and ego-building, you must resist the temptation and keep in mind that you are not a marriage counselor or a psychiatrist. You are not equipped to help these people solve their marital and family problems, and knowing about them in detail will do nothing but make you feel embarrassed, uncomfortable, and full of helpless sympathy. It is enough to know that a child's parents are having difficulties without needing to know the exact nature of the troubles.

After they have confided in you, feuding parents often try to get you to take sides. The child's mother naturally wants you to take her part and form a united front against her husband and, similarly, the husband wants you to join him in his fight against his wife. The child tends to be completely forgotten when the situation is allowed to come to this point. Be sympathetic, but do not commit yourself to anyone's point of view. Keep emphasizing that it is the youngster and only the youngster whom you are able to help, and your sole interest is in doing the best for him. Remind the parent, if necessary, that you are only able to work with the child during school hours, and that you can't provide special assistance when you are off duty. One mother once called me at home one evening, asking me to drive over and settle an argument she and her husband were having with their son. I declined as gracefully as possible, stating that I really couldn't do that, and there wasn't that much I would be able to accomplish if I went over there anyway.

One thing that *can* be done with parents who demand a more-than-reasonable amount of involvement and time is to arrange for a referral to the appropriate community agency. Agencies differ from community to community, but in most larger urban centers there are family service agencies, child guidance services, or psychological clinics. You do not have to give the impression that you are completely unconcerned about the outcome, for you still have the child in your class and have a responsibility to help him. Hence you can say that you will work through the school authorities in cooperating with the community agency on matters related to the learning problems and classroom behavior of the child.

It is essential to involve the principal and/or the school psychologist (or school social-worker) in such a referral. For one thing, such referrals lie in the area of community-school relations, in which these specialists have more expertise, experience, and responsibility than you do. For another thing, problems involving family disintegration are basically community problems, and community agencies should be put on notice that some kind of intervention may be called for to prevent social damage or at least keep it to a minimum.

16

PTA-ing and other wholesome activities

In some schools, attendance at Parent-Teacher Association meetings is compulsory for teachers. In other schools it is optional, or teachers take turns going. Although you may not look forward eagerly to returning to school for an evening session after a tiring day with still another to look forward to tomorrow, there is little joy expressed at faculty meetings when PTA-sponsored weekend events are announced.

Regardless of whether principal's decree or the prompting of a calvinistic conscience brings you to such meetings, the fact remains that they are a small but significant part of your professional role. Americans and Canadians are unlike parents of other countries in the extent that they are actively involved, if only around the fringes, in the educational programs of their children's schools. In the short range, this can be a nuisance but, in the long range, it works out to everyone's benefit. Parents are more eager to cooperate with teachers once they have an idea of what the school's program is about, and many a school bond-issue has been lost because schools and parents were estranged.

There are other small dividends as well. When you and your children attend weekend events, you appear more real and more human to them, and you can see them in a different setting, interacting with their parents, siblings, and playmates. The psychological bonds between you and the children are stronger because of this experience.

I suppose it is for the latter reason that I enjoy participating in school picnics and carnivals. Naturally, I avoid admitting this strange preference to my colleagues, even though I suspect that a number of them share this secret pleasure of mine. Teachers have been exploited so often and by so many that I suppose they must adopt a kind of a cynical pose, lest their colleagues become aware that they really enjoy these get togethers with children and parents away from school premises. If you really do dislike these affairs, no matter how well conceived they may be, try to shelve your resentment and make the best of it. At least you can feel very virtuous for weeks thereafter!

The best image to maintain at such public functions as PTA meetings and school picnics is one that is cheerful, friendly, interested, but noncommittal. This is not the time to allow a parent to engage you in an in-depth analysis of the child's problems. Really serious discussions are best done by appointment when you have your notes at hand and have done some preparation for the interview. However, some parents are very busy and hard to contact, so you may have to let your preference for the ideal interview situation go by the board and seize the opportunity to make a much-needed exchange of information with the elusive Mr. and Mrs. Green. But try to nail down a regular appointment so that a more complete interview can take place.

LET US BE KIND TO ROOM MOTHERS

One important function of the parents' organization is that of providing each teacher with one or more room mothers. Mothers who are not employed outside of their homes are recruited for this job. Their duties are usually confined to arranging class parties and collecting money for field trips but, in some schools, room mothers are encouraged to serve as teacher aides to help out in the classroom. You need to inform your room mother well in advance of any function where you will require her services. If you are planning a Christmas party for your children, alert the room mother at least two weeks in advance, or you may find yourself baking cupcakes and popping corn in the wee hours of the morning on the day of the party.

Many teachers treat their room mothers in a rather offhand manner, judging from some of the negative comments I have heard from these ladies. One mother in our school claimed she received a frantic phone call from a teacher during the afternoon preceding a Christmas party, requesting 60 cupcakes. The poor woman drove around looking for a market that was open after her house-guests and her children had been bedded down, and stayed up very late baking and frosting. When she dragged herself and her goodies over to school the next day, she was informed by this thoughtless teacher that she would have been better off to have made more Christmasy-looking cupcakes than the chocolate ones that were all she could come up with on such short notice. This lady brooded about this breach of manners for years, and I don't blame her!

WELCOME TO OUR HAPPY CLASSROOM

There are three annual events for which most public schools extend open invitation to visitors from the community: Back to School Night, Open House, and Public Schools Week. The events may go by different names in different communities, but almost every school has them in one form or another. The first one—Back to School Night—is usually for parents and teachers only. This is when you explain your instructional program to the parents and answer any of their questions about your philosophy of education or any other issues the parents may want to know about. Open House is generally held in the spring, and everyone—parents, children, and friends—is invited to view the classrooms and admire the children's work. During Public Schools Week, parents are scheduled to come and observe their child and his teacher in action during the regular school day.

I find Back to School Night to be the most nerve-racking and pressure-producing of the three situations. Back to School Night is very hard on teachers who are poor at public speaking, because they are expected to make some sort of speech to the parents on the nebulous topic of "My Educational Program and Goals." It is hard enough for many teachers to compose this little talk, in which you are expected to be witty, folksy, sensible, and inspiring, as well as competent, efficient, insightful, and self-assured. Until you have had some experience in presenting a standard message that represents your views, the experience can be, to say the least, upsetting.

Many neophytes, hoping to save themselves from having to hold forth for 15 minutes, try to involve their audience in a question and answer period, saying that they don't want to bore the parents with information that they are not interested in hearing. One problem with this approach is that most parents feel shy and awkward about asking questions and are not sure what they can or should ask the teacher. Or they may ask the wrong questions and show everyone how stupid they think they are.

It is better to give a brief talk on "What we do in the third grade," for examples in order to stimulate questions than to say blithely, "Just feel free to ask me anything you want to know about my program," and then sit back in silence while the assembled parents stare at you glumly. Hopefully your principal will circulate some suggestions for conducting a fruitful Back to School Night program. If he doesn't, ask the other teachers what they do.

I plan my talk beforehand, jotting down brief notes of what I plan to cover so that I am not in the position of delivering a canned speech. Keep the talk short and stay away from educational jargon and similar terms with which the parents may not be familiar. If you are using a new approach or curriculum in any subject area, you might want to explain the purposes and content of this to the parents. It helps to say how pleased you are with all the students in your class, and how you are enjoying working with such a fine group of children. This sets a nice tone to the proceedings.

Open House goes a lot more smoothly, because you already know most of the parents from conferences and other contacts prior to this event. You are also not expected to make a speech. Your job is merely to circulate, smile, and make small talk since the evening really belongs to the children. Most parents who attend Open House come with youngsters who are eager to show off their work and art projects to their appreciative parents. Parents usually have less time to corner you about their child's behavior or academic progress on this occasion, since they have to visit the classrooms of all their children in a short period of time. If this does happen, say what you can, but don't spend too much time with one set of parents, or the others will feel slighted.

If you have put your children to work arranging the room in an attractive manner, and have provided plenty of displays of student work, you have nothing to worry about. Stay away from phony, elaborate displays and projects that take away from classroom time prior to Open House Night. Most people don't notice or appreciate such things as a rule, and they won't know how much blood, sweat, and tears went into constructing that 12-foot dinosaur anyway.

THE OBSERVING PARENT

Parent observations of your lessons can produce tensions similar to the ones you might experience during your principal's visits. The difference is that the average parent is not as well informed as your principal about curriculum and teaching methods and really doesn't know what to look for. If the majority of the children are listening to you, and are industriously occupied, that is all that is needed to send the observing parent away feeling pleased about his visit. Schools often limit a parent's visit to 20 minutes, and if you feel a certain mother or father will be prone to planting himself in your classroom for hours on end, try to schedule his observation about 20 minutes before a recess or lunch period, in order to provide a natural break when you can chat with him briefly while tactfully sending him on his way. Some parents won't be bothersome, no matter how long they stay, but you usually don't know this beforehand. I had a delightful grandmother in my room for an hour and a half, during which time she helped out and became so interested in the lesson and its follow-up that she did the assignment right along with her grandson and his friends!

Have the child seat his parents wherever they wish to sit, and encourage him to share his books and materials with them. It is also appropriate to tell your class that George's mother will be coming to social studies this afternoon. This will alert them for the appearance of the strange person, and her arrival will be less disturbing. While the children are working, you can talk briefly to the mother, explaining anything that you feel is necessary. Encourage her to look around the room and move about freely. Thank her for coming when she leaves.

One teacher at my school has a very ingenious technique that she used for Public School Week. After she finds out which parents are interested and are able to come to school and observe their children, she schedules an individualized reading conference with the child during the time of his parent's visit. This gives the parent a chance to see his child in action, working on a one-to-one basis with the teacher. The reaction to this approach is universally favorable. The parent comes away feeling he knows exactly what his child is doing in reading, and he is also impressed by the fact that the teacher works with his child individually. The parent now knows what his child means when he says, "Today I had a reading conference with Mrs. Brooks," and he has seen how the conference is conducted. His child's skills and deficiencies show up bright and clear in these situations, too!

A FINAL WORD—MOSTLY POSITIVE

As you sally forth to conquer in your war against Ignorance, Immaturity, Irresponsibility, and all the other Is, you will find that you could not have chosen a more difficult profession. You make your entrance into the classroom, full of enthusiasm and high hopes, only to find yourself bogged down with thankless, annoying, trivial tasks and frustrations that are a part of every teacher's daily life. High-minded goals are often lost sight of as you get involved in the messy details of collecting milk money, filling out attendance sheets, pasting test scores in cum folders, and checking up on the fulfillment of behavioral objectives. There are seemingly endless recess duties, faculty meetings, and committee details, plus hours spent on lesson plans and on correcting papers.

With all this stress, strain, and tedium, one might suppose that teaching jobs would go begging. They don't, of course, and there are literally millions of individuals, qualified and otherwise, who would love to teach. There is no doubt of it: those of us who have the chance to teach are the lucky ones.

Why do we consider ourselves fortunate, and why is there such an overwhelming demand for teaching jobs? The answer to these questions seem obvious: all the major and minor annoyances that teachers must face are far outweighed by the magnitude of the personal rewards they can find in teaching. Indeed, the annoyances may even contribute to the attractiveness of teaching. Some psychologists tell me that the harder we work, and the more difficulties we overcome, in achieving our rewards and successes, the more they mean to us. If this is true, it provides at least one explanation of why teaching is so popular, and it helps explain some of the joy *I* get out of teaching. The successes I have are *never* easy: they *always* come after the children and I have worked hard to get them.

But there are other rewards as well. Teaching is interesting, varied, challenging and full of the unexpected—never a dull moment, to use a hackneyed phrase. And there is also the opportunity to love children and be loved in return. Few occupations, other than parenthood itself, offer such rewards.

As a result, we teachers get involved, sometimes in spite of ourselves, usually unaware of what is happening to us, in planning and carrying out our daily tasks, following through on our commitment to the development of young lives. This you will do, too. Most of the children will leave your class at the end of the year more mature, more knowledgeable, possessing more in the way of intellectual and social skills than when they came in September. To be sure, some of this will come from parents, friends, the adventures of life, and mere growing. But some vital part of it, perhaps more, perhaps less, will be due to you.

In a word, they will be richer for having known you.

Suggested Readings

Stephen E. Beltz, *How to make Johnny want to obey*. Englewood Cliffs, N.J.: Prentice-Hall, 1971. Dr. Beltz was, at one time, the executive director of the Center for Behavior Modification in Philadelphia. Although the book at times tends to overstress the importance of the reward as such, and is inclined to overlook the child's motives, it nevertheless presents behavior modification techniques in ways that make them understandable and useful for parents, teachers, and any adults who work with children.

Ronald D. Carter, *Help! These kids are driving me crazy*. Champaign, Ill.: Research Press. Another book on behavior modification, written in a lively style.

Siegfried Engelmann, *Preventing failure in the primary grades*. Chicago: Science Research Associates, 1969. Describes clearly, and in detail, procedures for helping children who have a history of failure in language and arithmetic skills.

Ken Ernst, *Games students play (and what to do about them)*. Millbrae, Cal.: Celestial Arts Publishing, 1972. Applies the principles of Dr. Eric Berne's "transactional analysis" to the kinds of psychological maneuvers that students engage in in order to establish and maintain patterns of behavior that are essentially immature and irresponsible. The book is at its best in helping teachers recognize the psychological motives that underlie the playing of "games."

Ira J. Gordon, *Studying the child in school*. New York: Wiley, 1966. Explains clearly, and in considerable detail, the ways in which teachers can gain better insight and understanding of children and their motivation, both as individual students and as classroom groups. The book is based on the principle that an effective teacher is a student, not only of pupil behavior, but of her own behavior as well.

Jacob S. Kounin, *Discipline and group management in classrooms*. New York: Holt, Rinehart, & Winston, 1970. Kounin is particularly good in his descriptions and analysis of "transitions:" the ways in which teachers move from the discussion of one topic or subject to another. Experienced teachers know that transitions present a number of problems: how to give the children a sense of completeness about the topic whose discussion is being terminated, how to get them to come to the right focus on the new topic, and how to keep the students moving together without losing any of them to boredom or confusion, and so on. Other topics treated are overdwelling, with-it-ness, overlapping, and the ripple effect in discipline.

Robert F. Mager, *Developing attitude toward learning*. Palo Alto, Cal.: Fearson Publishers, 1968. A down-to-earth little paperback that presents commonsense approaches to teaching-learning problems with the light touch. A book that any teacher can read with enjoyment and profit.

Dorothy M. McGeoch and others, *Learning to teach in urban schools*. New York: Teachers College Press, Teachers College, Columbia University, 1965. There are many books on inner-city education and its many problems, but most of them are *about* the problems. This book differs in that it is the account of the experiences of four first-year teachers, what they did that worked, what they did that didn't work, and how they felt about it all. Taken as a whole, it is a very encouraging and supportive book for those who teach or will be teaching in inner-city schools.

William C. Sheppard, Steven B. Shank, and Darla Wilson, *How to be a good teacher: Training social behavior in young children*. Champaign, Ill.: Research Press, 1972. This brief paperback is a handbook describing behavior modification techniques that teachers of young children have found to be useful. It is simple, detailed, and has many practice examples.

Sidney Trubowitz, *A handbook for teaching in the ghetto school*. Chicago: Quadrangle Books, 1968. Written by the principal of an inner-city school, this book contains many examples of the experiences and techniques that have been successful with children who live in a slum environment. The appendix contains an excellent list of books that black children have found to be interesting. A second list consists of books for teachers, some of general interest on such topics as how to role-play a story and others related to the historical and social background of minority-group people.

Index